Sew Smart ©

with

Ultra Suede® fabric

and other luxury suedes

by Clotilde and
Judy Lawrence

Fashion art by Bernard Schorr
Diagrams by Judy Lawrence

ISBN O-9605860-08

Sixth Printing - 1988

Published by
CLOTILDE, INC.
1909 S.W. First Avenue
Ft. Lauderdale, Fl. 33315

ABOUT THE AUTHORS

Clotilde

At the age of six, **Clotilde** picked up the needle and hasn't stopped sewing since. A graduate of Miami University, Clotilde worked in the wardrobe department of 20th Century Fox, and sewed commercially for boutique shops in Beverly Hills. This is where she learned many custom sewing techniques. Her curiosity about "how expensive designer clothes are sewn" was satisfied while making alterations on these garments. From this experience came many of the professional techniques found in *SEW SMART* and now *SEW SMART WITH ULTRA SUEDE® FABRIC.*

Clotilde

Clotilde taught sewing for many years at an exclusive fabric store in Woodland Hills, CA—covering all facets of sewing, from basic sewing to tailoring, to working with Ultra Suede fabric. For the past three years she has traveled extensively in the United States and England lecturing to several thousand women on the easy way to sew to achieve professional results.

A love of antiques and sewing culminated in combining the two areas by collecting antique sewing items. She has an extensive collection with some tools dating back 300 years.

Judy Lawrence

Judy began sewing as a young teenager and continued making her own and most of her family's clothes after she married and had children. She began her teaching career in the Los Angeles area in 1968 when she realized she needed some way to support her "fabric habit." Judy wrote her first book, *SEWING KNITS,* in 1970, and *SEWING KNITS MENSWEAR* in 1971. Both books won wide acceptance as texts for knit classes in fabric stores and schools throughout the United States and Canada.

Judy

Judy has worked as a consultant for many large companies involved in the home sewing industry, and has also written educational material for other publishers. She is well known as an author and lecturer, and has taught classes and conducted seminars all over the country. She met Clotilde at a teacher's workshop in 1970, and their friendship and professional experiences developed into the co-authoring of *SEW SMART* and now this new book, *SEW SMART WITH ULTRA SUEDE® FABRIC.*

TABLE OF CONTENTS

WHAT IS ULTRA SUEDE® FABRIC 1

BEFORE YOU BEGIN 2
   SELECTING PATTERNS.. 3
   SEAM VARIATIONS 5
   YARDAGE REQUIREMENTS 5

SEWING NOTIONS 6
   SCISSORS 6
   PINS 6
   THIMBLE... 6
   MACHINE NEEDLES 7
   THREAD 7
   IRON 8
   RULERS.. 8
   SEWING TAPES 8
   GLUE STICK 8
   LIQUID GLUE 8
   WATER ERASABLE MARKING PEN 9

MARKING THE FABRIC 9

SEAMS.. 10
   CONVENTIONAL SEAMS..................................... 10
   FLAT SEAMS 13
   STITCHING TIPS 15

INTERFACING... 17

LINING.. 20

CUTTING THE FABRIC 22
   GENERAL CUTTING TIPS.................................... 23
   FLAT SEAM CUTTING TIPS 26
   CUTTING SLEEVES 32
   CUTTING PANTS 34
   CUTTING LININGS 34

CONSTRUCTION TECHNIQUES 35
   DARTS 35
      Conventional Dart 36
      Lapped Dart 37
      Slot Dart 38
   POCKETS 38
      Patch Pockets 38
      Patch Pocket With Flap 40
      Slash Pocket With Flap 40

    Welt Pocket..44
    Single Welt Pocket With Flap........................46
    Double Welt Pocket..................................46
    Flap Pocket in Yoke Seam............................48

LININGS...50
  PARTIAL LININGS...51
  FULL LININGS..55
  SLEEVE LININGS..56

FRONT FACINGS...58
  FRONT BANDS...61
    Faced Bands...61
    Bands With A Cut-On Facing..........................63
  COLLARS...64
    Collar With A Separate Band.........................64
    Collar Without A Band...............................68
    Collar With A Cut-On Band...........................70
  SLEEVE VENTS..70
    Slash Vent..70
    Tailored Vent.......................................71
    Vent In A Seam......................................73
    Faced Vent..74
  CUFFS...76
    Cuff With A Separate Facing.........................78
    Fold-Over Cuff......................................80
  SETTING IN SLEEVES......................................81
  ZIPPERS...83
    Center Slot Zipper..................................83
    Lapped Zipper.......................................85
    Fly Zipper..87
  WAISTBANDS..89
    Faced Waistbands....................................90
    Fold-Over Waistbands................................91
  HEMS..93
    Conventional Hems...................................93
    Faced Hems..94
    Hems At The Front Facing............................95
  BUTTONHOLES...96

LEFTOVER PROJECTS..102
  WRAP BELT..102
  PATCHES..102
  BUTTONS..102
  BUTTONHOLES..102
  PIPING...102
  FASHION ACCENTS..103
  SWEATER TRIMS..105

TAILORED VENT PATTERN......................................109

Sew Smart with Ultra Suede fabric

Although the following instructions are for Ultra Suede® fabric they can also be used for other luxury suede fabrics, such as Lamous, that can utilize the flat method of construction.

ULTRA SUEDE® FABRIC

Ultra Suede fabric is easy to sew! Yes, that's really true! It's easier to use than most woven fabrics and lots of knits. One of the most luxurious fabrics available today, it is used extensively in high-fashion clothes by top name designers.

Why don't more people sew it at home? For one thing, it is quite expensive—$50 per yard—and most home sewers are afraid of making a mistake on such an expensive fabric. However, as soon as you read through these instructions, you will see that Ultra Suede fabric really is easy to sew, and those designer clothes that you have dreamed about can easily be yours at a fraction of their cost.

WHAT IS ULTRA SUEDE FABRIC?

Ultra Suede fabric is a non-woven fabric made from 60% polyester and 40% non-fibrous polyurethane. It does not have a lengthwise or crosswise grain, but it does have an up and down nap. Ultra Suede also has quite a bit of cross grain stretch, which is not true of all the other luxury suedes. It has all the advantages of real suede leather and none of the disadvantages.

It is completely machine washable and dryable and does not shrink. Washing makes the fabric softer and helps eliminate the "rustling sound" that it has when new. Wash in warm water and dry at medium heat, being careful not to overdry. Remove the fabric from the dryer immediately for best results. It is not necessary to pre-shrink this fabric.

Ultra Suede fabric can be dry cleaned if you prefer but it isn't at all necessary. Why make your fashion garment that much more

1

expensive with added cleaning bills if you don't have to? This is one of the fabric's big advantages over real suede. Note: While washing softens the fabric, dry cleaning preserves the original firm hand. If you want to retain a more crisp look, dry cleaning is the answer. Most ready-to-wear Ultra Suede® fabric garments are marked dry clean only. This is usually because non-washable linings and bindings have been used in the construction, not because the fabric is not washable.

Garments made from Ultra Suede fabric will not shrink, ravel, pill, peel, lose their nap, or crock (meaning the color doesn't rub off as with real suede). It is wrinkle proof and lightweight, making it ideal for travel. You won't feel "worn out" wearing an Ultra Suede fabric coat or jacket as you will with heavier, real suede garments.

Ultra Suede fabric is warm like a sweater, and it does breathe. You won't perspire in it as you will when wearing other fake leathers. It acts like a wind breaker—the same as real leather—so even though it is lightweight, it can be quite warm on a cool breezy day.

Jackets and coats made from the fabric are great for outerwear. A light-colored Ultra Suede fabric trench coat is a very practical item because it is so versatile and can be machine-washed and dried whenever needed. Outerwear garments can be made water repellant by spraying with Scotchgard®. This treatment also makes the lighter colors of suede somewhat dirt repellant.

Ultra Suede fabric doesn't water spot or stiffen when wet so you can spot-clean stains on any garment and not have to worry about left-over cleaning marks.

One word of caution—all synthetic suede fabric burns easily. A dropped cigarette ash can immediately leave a permanent mark or hole. Smokers, please be careful, and non-smokers, watch out for careless smokers at crowded parties.

BEFORE YOU BEGIN

Now that you know some of the facts about Ultra Suede fabric and are excited about this luxurious fabric, you should be ready to begin your own "Designer Fashion." But, before you rush out and buy your favorite shade, please **read through the rest of these instructions.** Some planning has to be done before you select the pattern and buy the fabric. Since Ultra Suede fabric does involve a sizeable investment, you should prepare yourself well in its cutting and stitching techniques. As was previously mentioned, Ultra Suede® fabric is easy to sew, but it is different from woven fabrics, and you should be well aware of the new methods before you begin.

SELECTING PATTERNS

Ultra Suede fabric looks best in jackets, vests and coats, and, of course, the traditional shirtwaist dress made so famous by Halston. It does not drape or ease well, so avoid patterns with close-fitting curves, lots of gathers or pleats and eased seams. Remember, Ultra Suede fabric is similar to leather, and garments that are casual and loose fitting, with tailored lines, look best. Styles calling for topstitching show the fabric to best advantage. Choose patterns with yokes, patch pockets and flaps, and extensive topstitching detail.

Ultra Suede is sometimes made up in pants, but before you purchase fabric for that purpose, find some ready-made pants to try on. Since you can not fit the fabric snugly, it can add pounds to your figure. The fabric will not hold a crease, although it is possible to stitch one in, and at least the upper portion of the pants must be lined to make them comfortable and durable. You might be better off finding a matching knit or woven fabric for pants and then use your money for another suede jacket.

There are some patterns available today that are designed for leather or leather-like fabrics. These have the lines that look best with suede-like fabric. You will find that the ease in the sleeve cap is less than normal, so the sleeve can be stitched into the armhole without any puckers.

Whether you use one of the leather-adapted patterns or a regular pattern, it is suggested that you make up a trial garment first so that any pattern alterations can be done before the fabric is cut. It is not practical to alter your garment after it has been cut and sewn due to some of the types of seam construction.

A heavy muslin can be used for the trial garment, but it's more fun to pick up a denim remnant to use. Denim is good for this purpose because it has the same drape and ease characteristics of the Ultra Suede fabric, and you will get a true picture of the fit and any construction problems you will have with the suede. Of course, a denim trial garment will cost a bit more, but with a little

more work you will have a wearable garment instead of just a muslin shell that you will throw away.

Things to look for when making the trial garment are length in sleeve and body, general overall fit, and suitability of the style. It's a lot easier to decide that you don't like a $6 or $8 denim jacket than it is to reject a $80 to $100 Ultra Suede® fabric jacket.

SEAM VARIATIONS

Look at ready-to-wear Ultra Suede fabric garments and you will notice different seam types used. Manufacturers use the conventional, topstitched, flat, and slot seams and you have the same options. Your choice will be governed by the desired finished look. Some garments are made using one seam method exclusively, while others are made with a combination of two seam types. For example, we saw a beautiful man's sport coat, by Halston, that was made with the conventional seam method except for the lapel, collar edges and pocket flaps. These were finished with just the cut edges topstitched together. This coat was also fully lined and was truly an elegant garment.

While all seam types work, we have found through experience that the flat method gives a smoother more leather-like look to the garment and saves you fabric in the pattern layout. The conventional seam is the one we recommend for armholes and can also be used for other seams except some method must be used to keep the seam pressed open flat if you are going to wash and dry the finished garment. We do not recommend conventional seam techniques for faced edges such as lapels, pocket flaps, etc. The edge will be quite bulky and tend to ripple after machine washing and drying. Read through the section on Seams to get more information on the various techniques.

YARDAGE REQUIREMENTS

Always check the amount of fabric needed before purchasing your Ultra Suede fabric. Yardage requirements given on pattern envelopes are usually more than actually required, and with the fabric being so expensive it doesn't make sense to buy more than you need. For example, a trench coat made from a Vogue pattern called for 4⅜ yards (3.9m) of 45" (115cm) fabric with a nap layout. The actual garment needed only 3¼ yards (2.9m) when the flat method of seam construction was used. The pattern wasn't shortened, so you can see how much fabric was saved. At $50 per yard that is quite a savings.

After you have completed your trial garment, made any pattern alterations, and decided on the seam method, you should then lay out the pattern pieces on a marked cutting board or another piece of 45" (115cm) wide fabric. Follow the layout tips given on page 24 to help position the pattern pieces and save fabric. Measure exactly how much fabric is needed and then go to the store to purchase your Ultra Suede® fabric.

SEWING NOTIONS

You don't have to use lots of special sewing notions when working with Ultra Suede fabric. However, we would like to review your usual sewing equipment, with some comments on a few items that can make construction easier.

SCISSORS
A good pair of sharp scissors is a must for cutting so that you get smooth rather than jagged edges. This is especially important when using the flat seam method since the cut edge is visible on top of the garment. Long, sharp, bent-handled shears will enable you to make smooth, long strokes for straight cuts. A pair of 6" (15cm) trimming shears is useful for the many trimming jobs involved with Ultra Suede fabric. Applique scissors make it easy to trim the underside of lapped seams without having to worry about cutting the garment.

PINS
Pins can be used without leaving holes as they do in real leather. Use sharp, dressmaker pins. The extra long pins (1½"/38 mm) with the large heads are excellent, as they can be pushed into the fabric much more easily than the small, metal headed pins. Regular pins will soon make your fingers feel as though they have holes in them.

A word of caution about pins. While you can use dressmaker pins in your Ultra Suede fabric with no left-over pin holes, this doesn't hold true for decorative pins or the pins used on the back of convention badges. Their large size will put holes in your garment.

THIMBLE
A well fitting thimble should be used to protect your finger. If

you are one of the many who say they have never been able to use a thimble, you will become an immediate convert. Ultra Suede® fabric is resistant to hand needles, and you need the help of a thimble to push the needle through.

MACHINE NEEDLES

Use a size 11/75 or 12/80 machine needle when sewing. If you use topstitching thread, you will have to go to a larger needle, probably a size 16/100.

Occasionally you may have some trouble with skipped stitches. Try using a needle one size larger of one of the Universal needles now on the market. Sometimes changing from one brand of thread to another will solve the problem. Increasing the pressure on the presser foot and/or using the straight-stitch throat plate with the small hole can also help. Product Note: Sewer's Aid helps eliminate skipped stitches.

Do not use leather machine needles.

HAND NEEDLES

Use fine hand needles when basting. As we mentioned above, a thimble is a must.

There are fine leather needles at most notions counters which penetrate Ultra Suede fabric much more easily than regular needles because they have a fine, sharp wedge at the point. These needles will really save your fingers. If you buy leather needles in a package of assorted sizes, use just the fine ones on your garment. The larger ones may leave marks in the fabric.

THREAD

Use polyester thread when sewing. It has good tensile strength. Regular size thread can be used for the flat seam method as well as the conventional seam method. Some of you may prefer to use topstitching thread for flat seams because of the heavier look it gives. That is fine if your machine can handle it, but there are some machines that just can't make good seams with this heavier thread. Make some seam samples using 4 to 6 layers of Ultra Suede fabric before beginning your garment to see how it is going to stitch. Sometimes topstitching thread will work on 2 layers of fabric but will balk at the thicker seams found at the neck, collar, pockets and flaps. You may have to decrease the bobbin tension when using this thread for both the top and bobbin thread. Ultra Suede fabric tends to grab the needle as it goes through the fabric, thereby throwing off the timing and causing skipped stitches and looping underneath. Don't be too concerned if you can't get good reults with topstitching thread. Regular thread looks just fine on Ultra Suede® fabric and works a lot easier.

IRON
Do not allow a bare iron to touch the Ultra Suede fabric. You will end up with an "iron mark." Always use a pressing cloth.

A Steamstress® iron is excellent for applying fusible interfacing and pressing seams as well as for applying fusible web for hems. Only a Steamstress can be used on the right side of the fabric and no press cloth is needed.

RULERS
A plastic "see through" ruler is a great help for the exact marking of seam allowances. The best kind to use is 2" (5cm) wide and 18" (45cm) long. It has red grid lines at ⅛"(3mm) intervals over the entire surface of the ruler.

SEWING TAPES
Double faced basting tape can be used during garment construction when making conventional seams instead of hand basting. Care must be taken in positioning the tape so it isn't in the stitching line. See page 10 for more instructions.

Product Note: Disappearing Basting Tape can be stitched through and disappears in the first washing. It's also excellent to eliminate "drag" when top stitching. We prefer the 1/8" width.

(pg. 206 SEW SMART)

GLUE STICK
A glue stick, available at art supply stores and many fabric stores, is a must when using the flat method of seam construction. This water soluble glue makes basting the seams quick and easy and even allows you to do some simple fitting with glued rather than stitched seams—great for fitting skirts. Product Note: We have found Dennison's Glue Stick or the Fantastic Baste & Glue Stick to be the best glue sticks when working with Ultra Suede fabric. Other brands are available but they don't seem to be sticky enough for this napped fabric.

LIQUID GLUE
Do not use liquid fabric glue on Ultra Suede fabric. It is not water soluble and will leave a permanent mark if you happen to get it on the right side of the garment.

WATER ERASABLE MARKING PEN

Another marking method suitable for this fabric is the water erasable marking pen. Marks put on either the right or wrong side of the fabric can be easily removed with a drop of clear water. The purple ink, air erasable pen fades automatically within 48 hours. So be sure to sew the seam before it disappears!

MARKING THE FABRIC

Construction marks should be transfered to the fabric wherever possible. Notches can be marked with small clips (never snip deeper than the notch) when seam allowances are left intact. Notches should be marked with a soft pencil, chalk or water erasable marking pen on the wrong side when the flat seam method is used. A sliver of hand soap can be used to mark construction marks on the right side of the fabric.

Other construction marks should be marked on the wrong side of the fabric and transferred to the right side of the garmet by running a threaded needle through the mark and leaving a long thread in the fabric.

When using the flat method of seam construction seamlines can be marked on the right side of the underneath layer with pins, Disappearing Basting Tape, Wheel-O-Chalk, or a sliver of soap.

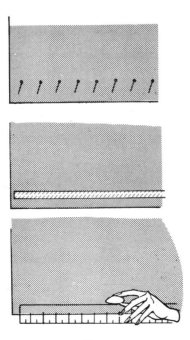

SEAMS

Most Ultra Suede® fabric seams should be basted together in some manner before they are machine stitched in order to prevent "creeping" of the top layer of fabric. This can be done by hand basting, use of a glue stick or double faced basting tape.

CONVENTIONAL SEAMS

If you choose to use conventional seams, you must be careful that the seams don't look bulky and unpressed when you finish. Special care must be taken to make all seams flat. Follow the instructions below to help you achieve this look.

Stitching Seams: Use one of the following methods when making conventional seams.

#1 Hand baste the seam together just inside the seamline. Machine stitch, holding the fabric taut. Remove the basting after the stitching has been completed.

#2 Tape-baste the two layers of fabric together using double-faced basting tape. Place the tape between the two layers of fabric about ⅛" (3mm) short of the seamline so that it will not be caught in the stitching. Machine stitch the seam, holding the fabric taut, and then peel away the tape in the direction of the nap.

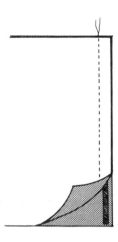

Finishing Seams: Ultra Suede® fabric will not hold a press through washing; therefore, it is impossible to press open a conventional seam and have it stay flat without some sort of help. This help is provided by fusible web or topstitching. We have seen some ready-made garments with just plain, pressed-open seams that looked very flat, and it made us wonder about the pressing problem. Perhaps the garment industry used some technique that we didn't know about. We decided to experiment a bit with some seam samples and found the following:

#1 It is possible to get very flat seams if you steam them open and then pound them with a clapper. Use a firm surface under the seam, rather than the padded ironing board, when pounding. A child's wooden block is ideal for this.

#2 These seams will not stay pressed flat through the washing and drying process. They will have to be steamed and pounded open after each washing. Sounds like a lot of work, doesn't it? Maybe it would be better to send the garment to the dry cleaners, and let him worry about it.

We have been unable to find a way of keeping these conventional seams pressed open without help, so we suggest that you use one of the following techniques.

#1 Place ¼″ (6mm) strips of fusible web under each seam allow-
    ance and fuse so that they stay flat. Make sure they are
    slipped at least ¼″ (6mm) away from the seam edge.

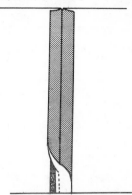

#2 Press both seam allowances to one side and topstitch
    through all layers. Stitch ¼″ (6mm) from the seamline, ⅛″
    (3mm) from the seamline or do two rows of topstitching, as
    shown.

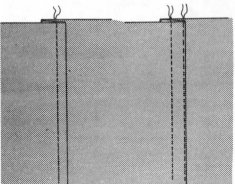

#3 Press open the seam allowance and then topstitch ⅛″ (3mm)
    from the seam on both sides.

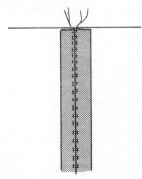

FLAT SEAMS

The flat method of seam construction gives a flat, "leather-like" look to your garment. It is very attractive and is the method used frequently on designer clothes. This method makes it easy to get that professional look with your first Ultra Suede® fabric garment, and it is also the fastest method of construction.

The flat seam is made by trimming away the entire seam allowance from one side of the garment piece and then overlapping the trimmed garment edge over the untrimmed seam allowance until the trimmed edge lines up exactly with the seamline. It is then basted by hand, tape, or glue, and stitched with two rows of topstitching. The seam line on the under layer of fabric can be marked using one of the methods given on page 9.

Basting Seams: When sewing multiple rows of topstitching on your garment, it is absolutely necessary to stitch each row from the same direction. Otherwise, the layers of fabric will "drag" against each other, causing ripples between the rows of stitching. Use one of the following methods when making flat seams.

#1 Hand Basted Seams: Baste the seams together approximately ¼" (6mm) from the cut edge. Position the basting stitches so that they won't be caught in the machine stitching. Do the first row of machine topstitching just slightly in from the cut edge, holding the fabric taut. Make the second row of stitching ¼" (6mm) away from the first, remembering to stitch in the same direction. Remove basting, and trim away the excess seam allowance from the wrong side. Holding the scissors at an angle to the fabric will make the trimming job easier.

#2 Tape Basted Seams: Place a strip of double-faced basting tape between the layers of the flat seam so that it is ⅛" (3mm) back from the top cut edge. Do the first row of topstitching just slightly in from the cut edge. Remember to hold the fabric taut. Carefully remove the tape. Make the second row of top-

Stitching ¼" (6mm) away from the first. Trim away excess seam allowance from the wrong side of the garment.

#3 Use Disappearing Basting Tape that can be stitched through and disappears in the first washing.

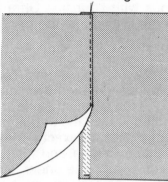

#4 Glue Basted Seams: Apply a glue stick to the wrong side of the fabric edge that has been trimmed. Keep the application about ¼" (6mm) wide. Overlap the trimmed and glued edge to meet the seamline of the other garmet piece; finger press in place and let dry for a minute. Secure the seam with two rows of top-stitching sewn in the same direction. Turn the garment to the wrong side and trim away the excess seam allowance. The narrow glue application will make this procedure easy because the under-edge will not be glued down. Wide glue application gives problems because you have to pull the fabric layers apart before you can trim.

Flat Seam II

This is an alternate flat seam technique that is used when putting in a center-slot zipper (see zipper instructions page 81), or when stitching darts.

Cut a 1" (25mm) wide strip of suede fabric as long as the seam or dart to be stitched. Position the suede strip under the garment pieces so that the trimmed edges of the seam or dart butt together in the center of the strip. Baste the seams together using one of the methods given in the previous flat seam section.

Make two rows of topstitching on both sides of the seam, making sure that all rows are stitched from the same direction.

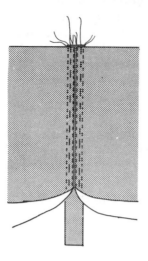

Since Ultra Suede® fabric will not hold a press, the above lapped seam is good to use on the front and back pants crease. Just cut your pattern apart on the front and back crease line and use the resulting four pattern pieces to cut the fabric.

Cut a 1" (25mm) wide strip of fabric that is long enough to go along each seam, and stitch the pant legs back together using the above technique. You will always have a sharp crease down your pant legs.

STITCHING TIPS

Sew with a slightly longer stitch length than usual—9 stitches to the inch or a stitch length of 3.5mm. Short stitches will weaken the fabric, and the stitch length tends to shorten when sewing Ultra Suede fabric. This problem can be solved by learning to stitch under tension (no, not you—the fabric). Hold the fabric in front of and behind the presser foot and keep it taut while stitching. Don't pull the fabric through the machine—just hold it with a slight tension so that it will feed evenly.

Multiple rows of stitching and all stitching on bands, cuffs, and belts must be sewn in the same direction because of the creeping problem.

Accurate topstitching is important for that professional touch. Done badly, it can ruin the look of the whole garment, and you can't afford that. Use your machine presser foot as a guide for even topstitching. The outside edge of most wide, zigzag feet is ¼" (6mm) from the needle. The inside edge of the right toe can also be used as an edge-stitching guide. Make some sample seams with your presser foot and see if it gives the measurements you need.

The seam guide on the throat plate of your machine can be used for wider lines of topstitching. If your machine does not have a seam guide, then make your own with a strip of wide adhesive tape placed to the right of the needle. Measure from the needle and mark the desired measurements on the tape.

The top layer of waistbands, front bands, and cuffs will tend to push ahead of the bottom layers even though you have basted everything together. This can be controlled by slipping a piece of fusible web, of equal width less ¼" (6mm), between the layers just before you do the topstitching. Fuse the layers together remembering to use a press cloth if you are using a conventional iron. This eliminates the creeping problem and also adds a bit of stiffness to these detail areas, usually eliminating the need for interfacing.

You may backstitch topstitched seams when using regular thread, or you may prefer to lockstitch the ends of seams. Some people prefer to tie thread ends. Never backstitch when using topstitching thread. Pull both threads to the wrong side and tie off in a square knot; leave 3" (7.6cm) thread ends, thread through a hand needle and weave the thread ends in between the garment and the facing fabric.

Topstitching Tip: When topstitching across thick seams (such as where the collar joins the neck) the machine tends to shorten the stitch length as it approaches the seam. Prevent this problem by following these steps: stop the machine when the front of the presser foot reaches the seam; lift the presser foot and place a folded strip of fabric or cardboard the same thickness as the garment under the presser foot, so that it becomes level with the thick part of the garment. Continue stitching until you have gone over the hump and then remove your "helper."

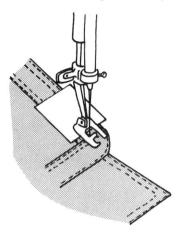

Spray the under side of the presser foot and the throat plate area of the machine with silicone to speed up and smooth the feed of the fabric. An aerosol spray form of silicone is available at most hardware stores.

INTERFACING

Interfacing is optional. If you want a soft look, don't use any. If you want a more structured look, use a fusible interfacing. Non-woven fusible interfacing works beautifully with Ultra Suede® fabric. Just remember not to use too heavy of an interfacing; otherwise your garments will look too stiff. Product note: we find Armo Weft or Whisper Weft to work very well.

Fusible interfacing must be pre-shrunk before applying to the fabric. This is easy to do with your steam iron before you trim any seam allowances. Place the cut-out interfacing piece, fusible side up, on the ironing board and steam it heavily. Hold the iron about ½" (13mm) above the surface, and don't let the iron touch the interfacing. Let the fabric cool completely before removing it from the board. A "shot of steam" iron is ideal for this technique.

Always test-fuse a piece of the interfacing to a piece of your fabric before applying it to the garment pieces themselves. Wash and dry the sample to make sure that the bond is strong and the interfacing doesn't pucker, and a line of demarcation doesn't show if you are only partially fusing a garment piece. Carefully follow the fusing instructions that come with your interfacing.

If you accidentally get some interfacing fused to the wrong place, or if the right side of the suede picks up some loose fusing material from the ironing board, you can remove it by gently rubbing the suede surface with denatured alcohol or paint thinner. Test first on a scrap of fabric to make sure it doesn't affect the color.

Fuse the interfacing to the wrong side of the part of the garment that shows, i.e., the lapel facing, the upper cuff and the upper pocket flap. Interfacing is usually applied to both the upper and under collars of tailored jackets, for extra support.

Use caution when applying interfacing to just part of a garment piece. A visible line of demarcation may show on the right side where the interfacing ends and the garment fabric continues. This is more apt to happen with light rather than dark colors.

Do not include interfacing in the seam allowances. Trim off an extra ⅛" (3mm) when using interfacing on garment pieces that have had the seam allowances removed so that a line of interfacing doesn't peak out between the two layers of fabric.

Trim the interfacing for the under collar only so that it is ¼" (6mm) smaller than the finished size of the collar around all edges so you won't have problems with peek-a-boo interfacing after the collar has been applied to the neck edge, rolled into position and stitched.

Under collars can have an extra piece of interfacing added just below the roll line, if desired. This gives more support to the collar stand. If you want a really firm collar finish apply interfacing to the upper collar as well.

EXTRA INTERFACING

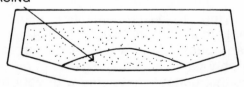

Lapels will not lie flat when the facing piece is completely inter-faced with a fusible. This problem can be solved by slashing the interfacing along the roll line, after you have fuse-basted it is several places; then complete the fusing process. Taping the roll line, as is done in other tailored garments, is not necessary with Ultra Suede® fabric.

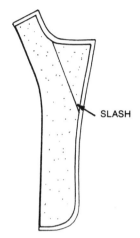

Another technique which can be used for turn-back lapels is to divide the interfacing at the roll line and apply it to the garment front and facing as shown. The interfacing should stop ⅛″ (3mm) short of the roll line on each garment piece.

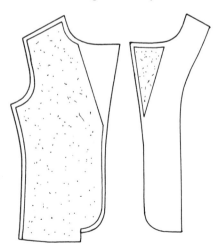

If you prefer, you can fuse interfacing to the entire front of the garment; just remember to trim the interfacing from the dart areas and slash it along the roll line. To give additional stability to the chest area of a man's jacket you can fuse interfacing to the garment front as well as the entire front facing. Cut the interfacing so it goes just to the first dart and then curves into the armscye as shown. Any line of demarcation left by the edge of the interfacing will be masked by the front dart and the patch pocket. A woman's jacket doesn't need interfacing on the jacket front—only on the facing.

Whether interfacing the garment or not, always back buttonholes with a square of woven interfacing or lining fabric in the same color as the garment. It is best to use a piece of matching lining fabric so that a white line of interfacing will not be visible in the buttonhole opening. Woven fabric will keep horizontal buttonholes from rippling or stretching. Non-woven interfacing is ineffective.

If you are unable to find a color-matched lining or interfacing fabric, camouflage the white in the buttonhole cut with a colored pen or pencil.

LINING

To line, or not to line, that is the question. Readymade Ultra Suede® fabric garments show a lack of uniformity in lining practices. Some Designer Fashions are fully lined, some are just partially lined, and some have no lining at all. In light of this confused state of affairs, we would like to give you some lining guidelines based on our experience of working with and wearing this luxury fabric.

Ultra Suede fabric is napped on both sides. While this doesn't present a problem in dresses and skirts, it does make putting on

20

jackets, coats and vests somewhat difficult. You will really get "hung up" if you try to pull on an unlined Ultra Suede® fabric jacket over a sweater. Linings will solve this problem for you and make your garment so much more comfortable to wear.

Ultra Suede fabric will show wear at points of strain (around collars, at elbows, and across shoulders) and where it is subjected to repeated chaffing (in underarm and crotch areas). Lining will strengthen these parts and prolong the life of the garment. Linings also cover up inside construction details such as welt pockets and darts on blazer-type jackets and men's sport coats.

The area at the top of the shoulder where a woman places the strap of her shoulder bag will show wear after a period of time. Carry a different bag or hold the strap in your hand when wearing your Ultra Suede fabric garment in order to prevent this.

After considering all the above observations, we definitely feel that linings (full or partial) should be used in Ultra Suede fabric coats, jackets and vests. Why some Designers line and others don't we can't explain, but your garment will be more comfortable to wear and more attractive if you take the time to add some lining. Also, when you consider the cost of your garment, it just makes sense to add lining if that means extending the life of your expensive investment. Follow the suggestions below for linings:

Full linings are recommended for coats and jackets having inside construction details that are best covered up, i.e., darts and set-in pockets.

Full linings can be used wherever desired for appearance's sake.

Vests should be fully lined for comfort. Ultra Suede fabric vests in better stores have just the fronts cut from suede. This type of vest is designed to be worn under jackets. The lining back allows the jacket to slip easily over the vest. Ultra Suede fabric can be used for the back of vests that are to be worn without a jacket.

Partial linings, consisting of the upper back and sleeve lining, can be used on jackets for both men and women. Jackets with front and/or back yokes are especially adaptable to partial linings because only the yokes are lined, and the yoke seams are neatly covered by the lining.

Ultra Suede fabric pants are more comfortable if they are lined, and the lining will prolong the life of the garment. Unlined, snug

pants will split out at the seat. Make a full length "drop lining" (attached only at the waist and zipper), using the pants pattern to cut the lining pieces. Or you can just make a short lining that extends only a couple of inches below the crotch.

All jacket and coat sleeves should be lined for comfort and strength. Elbows will soon wear through unlined sleeves if the garment is worn often. If this happens, you can save the garment by adding hunting patches to the elbow area in a matching or contrasting color of Ultra Suede® fabric.

Lining Fabrics

Fabrics suitable for lining Ultra Suede fabric garments are light-weight polyester lining fabrics that are machine washable and dryable. Look for something that has a fairly slick surface so that it will slide over your other clothes easily. Lining fabrics should be pre-shrunk before cutting.

Some suggested fabrics are: a la creme, Caio, some of the pretty printed Ultressas and even woven, lightweight Qianas.

CUTTING THE FABRIC

The method of seam construction that you use on your Ultra Suede fabric garment will influence the amount of fabric needed and the pattern layout. The flat seam method uses less fabric than the conventional seam method because seam allowances are removed from some sections of the pattern. This enables you to place the pattern pieces closer together on the fabric.

You should buy your pattern and make up the trial garment even before you buy your fabric so that you will have all the length alterations done and will have decided on the method of seam construction. If you are going to use the flat seam method, you should fold the affected seam allowance out of the way and make a trial layout on your cutting board or another piece of 45" (115cm) wide fabric. This will give you an accurate measurement for your yardage and will probably save you quite a bit of money.

GENERAL CUTTING TIPS

Whether you choose the flat or conventional seam method, all pattern pieces should be placed on the fabric so that the tops face the same direction (nap layout). If you cut with the nap running up the pattern pieces, you will get a richer color. If the nap runs down, it will give a lighter, glossy look. The choice is yours—just make sure your placement of the pattern pieces is consistent. After repeated washings the nap direction seems to disappear, but initially there is quite a difference. You can "cheat" a bit on the nap with small pattern pieces. These can be tilted off grain if necessary in order to get a better fit on the fabric.

Ultra Suede® fabric can be cut double. Fold the fabric wrong side out and pin the pattern pieces in position. Mark the wrong side of each cut piece with a strip of drafting tape, soap, chalk, or soft pencil immediately after it has been cut to help you in the construction process. Position the tape strips so that they will not be caught in any machine stitching.

Mark garment pieces that have not had the seam allowance trimmed with small clips at the seamline on each end of the seamline. These clips will remind you of what has or hasn't been trimmed when you put the garment together.

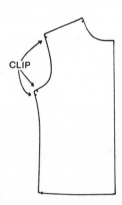

Bias markings on pattern pieces can be ignored. This is a big fabric saver. Place bias pattern pieces on the cross-grain to give them a bit of stretch.

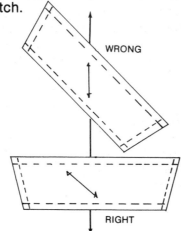

Eliminate the center back seam if it appears on your undercollar pattern. Just cut the pattern on the cross grain—it has enough stretch.

Cut all collar and cuffs on the cross-grain so they will match the nap of the rest of the garment. Positioning all pattern pieces on the fabric with the printing running in the same direction will give you the correct layout.

Waistbands should be cut on the cross-grain whenever possible. Some men's jacket patterns, calling for a waistband finish, will be too large to cut the band crosswise. You will have to piece the band at the side seams or cut the band lengthwise on the fabric. Belts should be cut lengthwise if they are longer than 45" (115cm). Always cut long lengthwise pattern pieces first so that you will know how much fabric you have left for the other pieces.

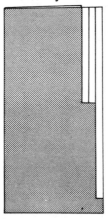

Sleeve and garment lengths should be adjusted before pinning the pattern to the fabric. (That's what the trial garment is for.) Trim hem allowances to ¾" (19mm). If you are going to make a conventional hem, the allowance will just be turned up and stitched or fused in place. If you are going to make a faced hem you should fold up the entire hem allowance before pinning the pattern to the fabric. Then cut ¾" (19mm) wide strips of suede fabric to face the hem edges. If the hem edge is curved, the facing strips must be cut following the same curve. Make sure you allow for enough fabric to cut the facing strips. Hem widths for garments that are going to be fully lined should be 1¼" (31mm) wide. Dress and skirt hems can be left at 2" (50mm) and hand stitched using a blind tailor's hem.

FLAT SEAM CUTTING TIPS

When using the flat seam method, fold back the affected seam allowances on the pattern pieces before you pin them to the fabric. Figuring out what is going to lap over what is somewhat like working a puzzle, but it is fun to do and isn't difficult if you follow the guides given below. A good rule to follow when figuring this out is to trim away the seam allowance of the pattern piece on which you will do the topstitching. Note: When pattern pieces show a topstitching line, that seam allowance is the one to be eliminated. Generally, it doesn't matter how you lap the seams, just be consistent within the garment.

Back shoulder seams are usually lapped over front shoulder seams. Trim away the back shoulder seam allowances. If the back shoulder seam includes a dart you may prefer to lap front over back.

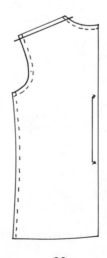

Yoke seams are always lapped over the body of the garment. Trim away the yoke seam allowances.

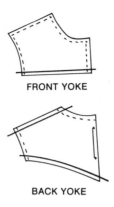

FRONT YOKE

BACK YOKE

Side seams are usually lapped front over back. Trim away the side seam allowances on the front pattern pieces.

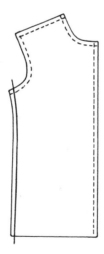

Garments with underarm bust darts should usually have the back side seam trimmed so that you can lap back over front. This will hide the multiple layers of fabric at the end of the dart. However, if there is a side pocket in a seam you must lap front over back.

Garments with front and/or back panels should have the seams lap front over back at each seam line. Trim away the seam allowances from the seam line closest to the front of the garment.

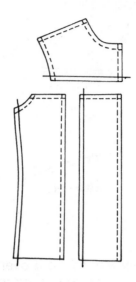

Waistbands, front bands and cuffs overlap the body of the garment. Their cut edges are topstitched together rather than conventionally stitched and turned. Trim away all the seam allowances from these pieces.

Important Sanity Saving Tip:

Facings for waistbands, front bands and cuffs should also be trimmed, but leave ⅛" (3mm) of the seam allowance around the outside edges. Leave the complete seam allowance at the edge that joins the body of the garment. This edge will be trimmed after being machine stitched in place. The ⅛" (3mm) allowance around the outside edges will give you some extra fabric to work with when you do the final rows of topstitching. This "extra" helps you make sure that you always catch the underside when stitching and saves your sanity. Other instructions will have you trim both seam allowances equally, but then it is easy to lose the under-edge when topstitching.

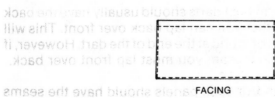

FACING

Patch pockets and patch pocket flaps should have all the seam allowances trimmed away. Leave a ⅛" (3mm) allowance on the flap facing for the above reason.

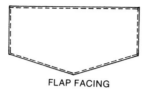

FLAP FACING

Facings for pocket flaps are usually cut from the same pattern piece as the flap itself. However, if you are short of fabric you can just cut a narrow facing for the pocket, as illustrated. Remember to leave a ⅛" (3mm) allowance on the outside edges of the facing for ease of construction.

Square flaps can be cut with the lower seamline on a fold, if you have large enough pieces of fabric to accommodate this size pattern piece. Trim the seam allowances from the outside edges of the pocket. Make sure the pocket nap goes in the proper direction when stitchig the flap in place.

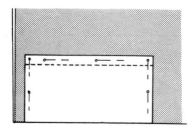

Pocket flaps that will be sewn into yoke seams should have all their seam allowances trimmed except for the seam allowance that will go into the seam. The flap facing should be trimmed the same way, only leave a ⅛" (3mm) allowance around the outside edges.

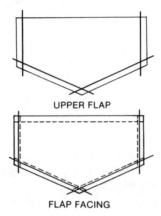

UPPER FLAP

FLAP FACING

For outerwear garments cut the pocket lining pieces from suede fabric if you have enough fabric. This looks nicer than using lining fabric, especially if the coat is to be only partially lined. It also feels good when you put your hands in your pockets. Use lining fabric for blazers and dresses.

One-piece collars or collars with a cut-on band should have the seam allowances trimmed from all four edges of the upper collar. Leave all the seam allowances intact on the under collar.

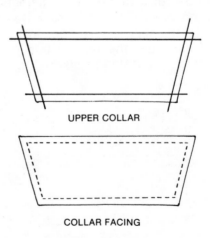

UPPER COLLAR

COLLAR FACING

Upper collars that have separate bands should have all the seam allowances except the lower edge trimmed. Trim the collar facing the same except leave a ⅛" (3mm) allowance around the outside edges. The band that goes inside the neck of the garment should have all the seam allowances trimmed away. Leave the seam allowances intact on the outside band, for ease in stitching and placement.

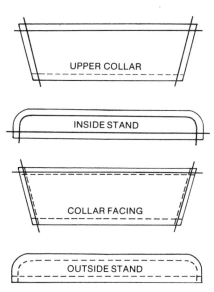

Front opening garments that do not have a separate front band should be cut without the front seam allowance. The facing for this garment piece should have the seam allowances trimmed to just ⅛" (3mm).

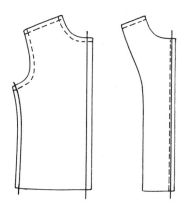

If you are not going to line or partially line the front of a garment with a front band finish, then you should modify the shape of the band facing as illustrated. This will help prevent wear at the front neck edge, as this area is a point of strain and will need some extra protection.

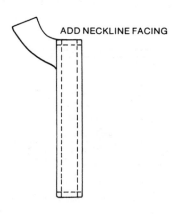

ADD NECKLINE FACING

Patterns having a straight edge at the center front, with either a band finish or a regular finish, can have the facing or band cut all-in-one so that you have a fold along the front edge rather than a cut edge. Overlap the front seamlines of the two pattern pieces and tape in place, as shown, before placing the pattern on the fabric. This method may create some layout problem because of the size of the pattern piece, so work it out before you buy your fabric.

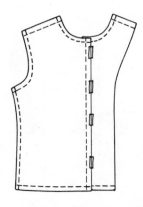

Garments without collars should have the neckline seams trimmed away. The neckline facing should have the neckline seam trimmed to ⅛" (3mm).

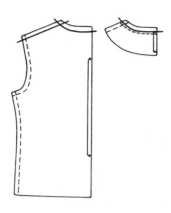

Front opening garments with a turn-back lapel and collar should have the edge at the top of the lapel trimmed to the point where the collar joins the neck edge. Trim the entire seam allowance from the garment front but leave a ⅛" (3mm) seam allowance around the edge of the facing.

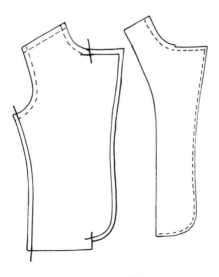

Corners that are to be sandwiched between cuffs, collars, and bands should be trimmed as shown.

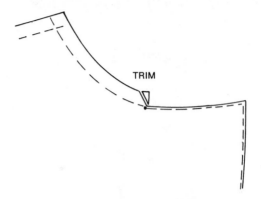

TRIM

If you are making a two piece sleeve and are using the flat seam method then eliminate the seam allowance on both sides of the upper sleeve and leave it intact on both sides of the under sleeve.

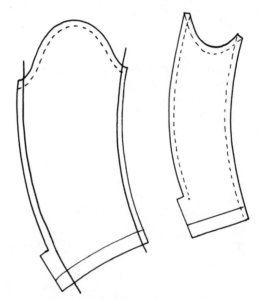

CUTTING SLEEVES

Whether you choose to use the conventional or flat seam method on your Ultra Suede fabric garment, the sleeve will be sewn into the armhole with a conventional seam. This technique is easier than trying to lap the armhole seam, and it gives a nicer look. Do not trim seam allowances from the armhole.

Since luxury suede fabric is difficult to ease, you must check the amount of sleeve cap ease allowed in the pattern and reduce it to no more than 1" (25mm). Note: Patterns designed for real or fake leather probably will have this excess ease already removed, but it is a good idea to double check before you cut out the sleeves.

Determine the pattern ease allowance by overlapping the front and back pattern pieces until the shoulder seams line up; pin in place. Walk a tape measure around the armscye seamline, from the underarm seam to underarm seam. This is easy to do if you place the tape measure on edge. Make a note of this measurement.

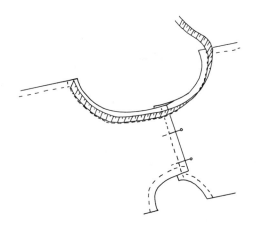

Now measure around the sleeve seamline, from underarm seam to underarm seam, with the tape measure on edge. The difference between the two measurements is the allowed sleeve-cap ease.

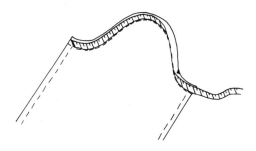

Cut the sleeve pattern apart where the armscye and underarm seams meet. Make two to six slashes in the sleeve cap, as shown. Make one slash for each ¼″ (6mm) of ease you need to remove.

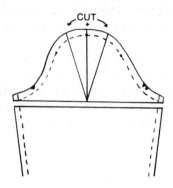

Overlap each slash up to ¼″ (6mm) and pin. Recheck the sleeve measurement and adjust the slash overlaps until you have the right amount of ease. Tape the slashes in place; tape the sleeve back together, and use this altered pattern to cut the suede.

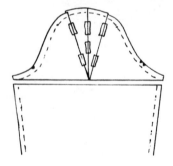

Note: Sleeve lining pattern pieces should be altered the same as the garment sleeve pattern.

CUTTING PANTS

The crotch seam of pants should be sewn with a conventional seam rather than a lapped seam. This is easier to do and more comfortable to wear. The lapped seam method can be used for all other pant seams.

CUTTING LININGS

Cut your lining from the lining pattern pieces or from the appropriate garment pattern pieces if separate lining patterns are not given.

Cut the underarm seamline of the sleeve lining ½" (13mm) higher than the garment seamline. This allows for the ease needed to cover the underarm seam allowance.

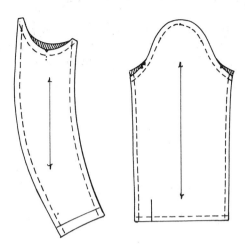

Before you cut your fabric, carefully review your pattern pieces to make sure you are lapping things properly. A little extra time spent at this point can save you from making a costly mistake.

CONSTRUCTION TECHNIQUES

Now that your garment is cut out, you are ready to start the fun part. Watching this fabulous fabric turn into a High-Fashion garment through your sewing skills is very exciting. You will be surprised at the ease and speed of the construction, so let's get started.

DARTS

Darts in Ultra Suede® fabric garments should be long, gradually tapering to a point. Short, wide darts are difficult to stitch without getting a pucker at the point. Patterns for skirts and pants that use yokes instead of darts are better choices for this fabric than patterns with conventional darts.

There are many ways of handling darts. Try all methods on scraps of fabric to see how they work and how they look. Select the method you find most suitable for your particular fashion.

Conventional Darts

Stitch the dart, gradually tapering to the point, and then use one of the following methods to finish the dart.

#1 Slash open the dart along the fold and trim to ½" (13mm). Press open and pound the seam flat. Hold the seam allowance in place with thin strips of fusible web.

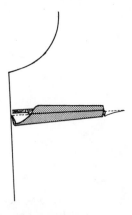

#2 Slash the dart open and topstitch along each side catching a 1" (25mm) square of fabric at the point of the dart as shown. This helps fill in the point of the dart and makes both sides equal.

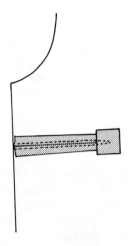

#3 Press the dart to one side and pound. Topstitch approximately ⅛" (3mm) from the seamline. You can stitch just one side or along both sides. This method looks nice on long, double ended darts on jacket fronts. Fill in the end of this dart with a square of fabric.

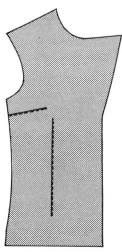

Lapped Darts

Skirt and pant darts and the darts at the back of the neck or shoulder can be cut open along one side, lapped, and double stitched in place. This method should be used only on fairly narrow darts because it is difficult to get a smooth point if the dart is very wide.

A small scrap of suede fabric added to the underside of the dart point, as previously described, will make the dart end smoother.

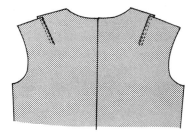

Slot Dart

The Slot dart method is the best choice when stitching a wide dart such as the ones found in some vest patterns. It can also be used for regular size darts if you desire the slot look.

Cut out the dart along the stitching lines. Bring the cut edges together and baste them to an inch wide strip of suede cut 1" (25mm) longer than the dart opening. (Glue stick works wonders here.) Topstitch along the dart edges with one or two rows of stitching, making sure the dart edges stay butted together.

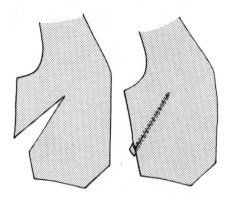

POCKETS

You will find many different types of pockets on the patterns that you might select for your Ultra Suede® fabric garment. Some will be more suitable to this fabric than others. Patch pockets with or without flaps are ideal, and the welt pockets described below will give a flatter appearance than welt pockets made with traditional stitching techniques. All the pockets are made wtihout any turned under or faced edge for the leather-like look.

You can easily modify the pockets given in your pattern so that they utilize the following techniques.

Patch Pockets

If a buttonhole is to be placed at the top of the pocket, make sure the pocket hem is wide enough to extend below the lower end of the buttonhole. The buttonhole needs two layers of fabric plus a patch of woven lining for support.

Cut the pocket without any seam allowances. Trim the upper edges of the patch pocket hem as illustrated. This prevents the edge of the hem from peeking out along the side of the pocket after it has been stitched in place. This is important for a pocket without a flap to cover the top edge.

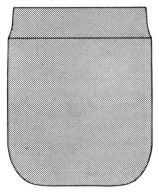

Fold over the hem allowance at the top edge of the pocket. Baste or glue in place and do two rows of topstitching across the top of the pocket. Another two rows of stitching can be done across the bottom edge of the hem if desired for a band effect. Remember to make all rows of stitching from the same direction.

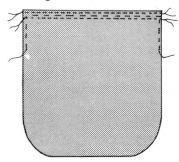

Base or glue the pocket in position on the garment and stitch in place with two rows of topstitching. Reinforce the top corners of the pocket with back stitching or decorative stitching.

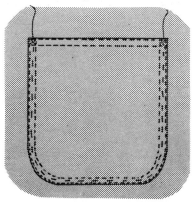

Patch Pocket With Flaps

Construct and apply the pocket as directed above.

Cut the pocket flap and facing as given on page 29. Baste the facing to the pocket flap, wrong side together, so that ⅛" (3mm) of the facing extends all around the edge of the flap.

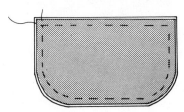

Do two rows of topstitching around the three outside edges of the flap. Trim the facing even with the flap edges.

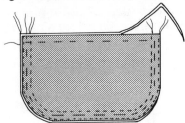

Baste or glue the flap in position on the garment and topstitch in place.

Slash Pocket With Flap

This pocket flap will have the full seam allowance left on the bottom edge of the flap and facing so that it can be sewn into the pocket slash. The pocket flap should be made before the pocket opening is cut so that the slash can be cut to fit the flap exactly. This procedure makes sure that no gaps are left at the sides of the pocket opening.

Flap Construction: Baste or glue the facing to the flap, wrong sides together, and topstitch 5/16" (8mm) from the edge, around the three sides, as illustrated.

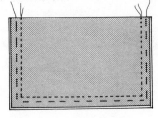

Edgestitch only the front edge of the flap. The sides will be edgestitched later. Trim the facing even with the edges of the flap.

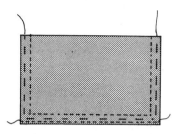

Mark the seam allowance on the right side of the flap with a strip of drafting tape. Be sure that the edge of the tape is right along the seam line, and both sides of the flap below the tape are exactly the same length.

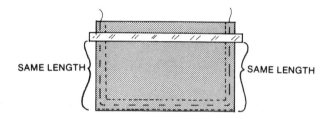

Pocket Construction: Cut along the pocket opening with an Exacto knife or single-edge razor, placing a pin at the end of each side of the opening to prevent overcutting. Make sure that the opening is exactly the same length as the finished flap.

Slip the flap into the pocket slash so that the tape lines up with the cut edge of the slash. Baste or glue the flap in position and remove the drafting tape.

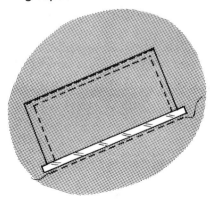

Topstitch the ends and across the width of the pocket through all the layers of the pocket flap and garment.

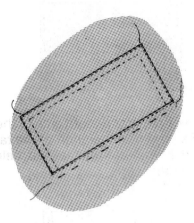

Pocket Lining: The pocket lining looks nice if Ultra Suede® fabric is used rather than lining fabric, especially if you are not going to fully line the garment. If the lining pattern is one long piece, it can be cut along the foldline to facilitate the use of small scraps of fabric. You can even alter the shape of the lining pieces to take advantage of the suede scraps. Cut the pocket lining pieces without seam allowances if you use Ultra Suede fabric.

Baste or glue and stitch one pocket lining piece to the seam allowance of the flap.

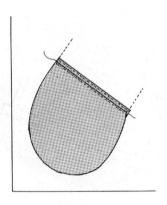

Working on the wrong side of the garment, cut two diagonal lines as shown, underneath the flap. Cut right to the stitching line, cutting the garment fabric only.

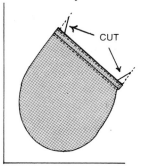

Lap the other pocket lining piece ¼" (6mm) over the free edge of fabric and baste or glue in position.

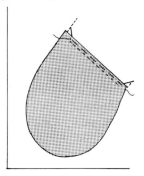

Turn the garment right side up and fold back the lower part of the garment until you see this basted seam. Machine stitch across the top of the lining piece.

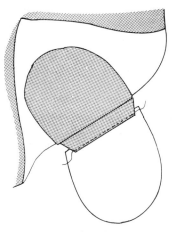

Baste or glue the pocket lining pieces together and edge-stitch.

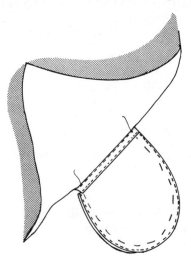

If the slash pocket is made on a garment with a front opening and facing, the pocket lining should be tucked between the facing and garment and tacked to the facing to keep it in place. Now, wasn't that easy? This is beautiful when used on a coat—make the finished flap 2″ (50mm) wide by 7″ (17.5cm) long.

Welt Pocket

This pocket is usually used for vests, but it can also be used as a chest pocket or hip pocket on a skirt, dress or pants.

Welt Construction: Delete the welt pattern piece and add 1″ (25mm) to the top of the pocket lining pattern. Cut this altered lining pattern from Ultra Suede® fabric, making sure the turned down portion of the welt has the correct nap direction. Cut one pocket piece minus the added 1″ (25mm).

ADD 1″ (25mm)

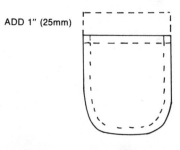

Turn down the 1" (25mm) welt extension, wrong sides together, baste or glue and do two rows of top stitching along the fold.

Pocket Construction: Cut along the bottom and side lines of the pocket markings with an Exacto knife or a single-edged razor. If you are making matching pockets, you must make sure that these pocket cuts are positioned and sized identically.

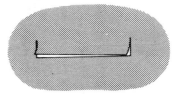

Slip the edgestitched welt into the slash, centering it in the opening. The right side of the welt should be against the wrong side of the garment. Baste or glue the welt in position. Edgestitch the sides and across the bottom of the welt.

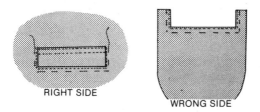

RIGHT SIDE

WRONG SIDE

Baste or glue, and stitch the other pocket lining piece to the wrong side of the flap of the garment that extends down behind the stitched welt.

Baste or glue and edgestitch together the outside edges of the pocket lining pieces.

47

Single Welt Pocket With Flap

Construct the welt pocket using the above instructions, but make sure the welt and pocket opening are just ½" (13mm) wide.

Make the pocket flap following the instructions for the patch pocket flap. The finished flap should be ½" (13mm) longer than the pocket opening. This extra ½" (13 mm) makes sure that the pocket opening will be completely covered by the flap.

Baste or glue the flap in position above the pocket opening and topstitch in place.

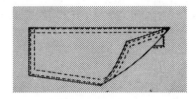

Double Welt Pocket

Use buttonhole method #3 on page 95 when doing a double welt pocket, except cut the pocket opening ½" (13mm) wide and as long as indicated on the pattern. Cut three suede strips 2" (5cm) wide and 1" (25mm) longer than the pocket opening.

Prepare two of the strips as described for the buttonhole. Slip a pocket lining piece between the layers of the lower welt strip, after the strips have been basted together and pressed open. Hand or glue baste the lining in place.

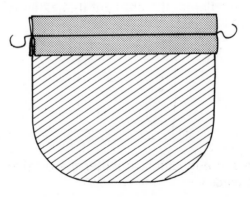

Center the prepared strips behind the pocket opening and hand or glue baste in place. Edgestitch around the pocket opening using a zipper foot, if desired, for greater visibility.

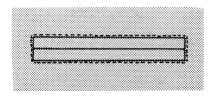

Stitch the remaining suede strips to the top of the other pocket lining piece lapping the suede ¼" (6mm) over the lining, and edgestitch.

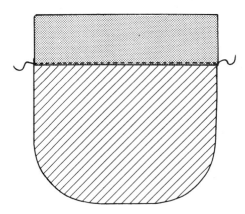

Position the lining/suede piece behind the pocket opening so the top of the suede strip is even with the top edge of the upper welt strip. If the lower edge of the pocket lining doesn't match, don't worry; just trim it even after the pocket is completed.

With the right side of the garment up, fold down the garment to expose the seam allowance of the upper welt strip. Hand or glue baste this seam allowance to the suede strip at the top of the second lining piece. Machine stitch across the seam allowance, catching the top of the pocket piece underneath.

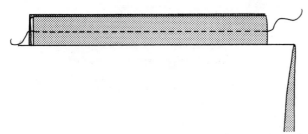

Fold over the side of the garment to expose the sides of the pocket lining pieces and close the pocket by stitching down the side, across the bottom, and up the other side.

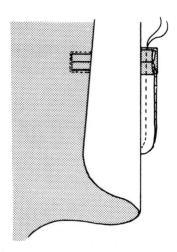

Flap Pocket in Yoke Seam

This flap pocket is a snap to make and can be used in the yoke seams of jackets, coats, dresses, and even pants.

Flap Construction: The flap and flap facing should have the top seam allowance left intact. The other seam allowances are completely trimmed from the flap and trimmed to just ⅛" (3mm) on the flap facing.

Baste or glue the flap and facing wrong sides together and do two rows of top stitching around the outside edge. Trim the facing edges even with the flap.

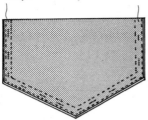

Pocket Construction: Cut two pocket lining pieces from Ultra Suede® fabric for each pocket, measuring at least 1" (25mm) wider than the pocket opening. Position one pocket piece on the garment, wrong sides together, centering it over the pocket marks. Baste or glue in place. Stitch an opening ½" (13mm) shorter than the finished measurement of the pocket flap, and ⅞" (22mm) deep. Make two rows of stitching and then trim the opening close to the stitching line.

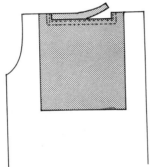

Position the other pocket piece so that the wrong side is against the right side of the first lining piece. (It looks nicer to have the right side of the fabric visible on the inside of the garment if it isn't going to be fully lined.) Baste or glue and edgestitch the pocket pieces together.

Baste or glue the flap in position, centering it over the opening. Mark the seamline, and baste the yoke over the flap. Stitch the yoke seam with two rows of topstitching.

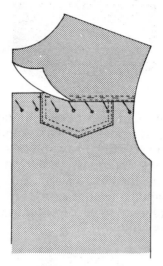

LININGS

Lining Ultra Suede® fabric garments makes them easier to slip in and out of, as well as prolongs the life of the garment. Coats, jackets, and pants should definitely be fully or partially lined and dresses and skirts can be lined or not, as you desire.

If you choose to fully line dresses, skirts or pants, attach the lining at the neckline and zipper for dresses, and at the waistline and zipper for skirts and pants, using traditional lining techniques.

Coats look best when fully lined. Jackets can be either fully or partially lined. The type of jacket lining you choose is a matter of preference, though patterns calling for front and back yokes are more suitable to the partial lining technique than patterns without yokes.

If you are going to fully or partially line your garment and the pattern gives a back neck facing, eliminate that facing and extend the lining all the way up into the neckline. Do this by pinning the facing pattern to the back lining pattern so the seamlines are directly on top of each other. Add extra width at the center back of the facing to allow for the back pleat. Cut the lining fabric from this altered pattern. This gives a much nicer finish to the inside of the garment and saves some fabric.

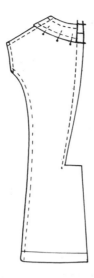

Stitching Tip: When stitching lining fabric to suede fabric do so with the lining up and the suede next to the feed dog. Hold both layers taut as you stitch and you won't gt any puckers.

Partial Linings

Partial linings consist of a full sleeve lining and a lining at the upper portion of the back and/or front of the jacket. If your pattern has front and back yokes, it is an easy matter to line just the yokes, cutting the lining pieces from the yoke patterns. Yoke linings are a good way to make a partial lining because the lower edges of the lining pieces are neatly enclosed in the yoke seams rather than hanging free. Follow the instructions below for yoke linings.

Patterns With Straight Yokes: Prepare the jacket for the lining by lapping the yoke over the body of the garment and basting the seam in place.

With the jacket wrong side up, place the yoke lining in position as shown so that the lining seamline is directly on top of the garment seam line. The right side of the lining is against the wrong side of the garment. Baste in place.

Turn the garment to the right side and edgestitch the yoke to the garment.

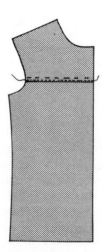

Working on the wrong side, trim the seam allowance to ⅜" (9mm). Fold the lining up into the finished position, wrong sides together, and pin.

Do the second row of topstitching on the right side of the jacket.

Only one row of stitching will show on the lining and the seam will be neatly enclosed.

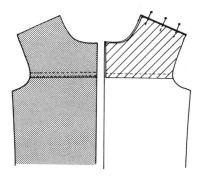

Baste the front yoke lining to the garment at the shoulder. Overlap the back shoulder over the front, leaving the back lining free. Baste the shoulder seam and machine stitch with two rows of topstitching.

Fold under the back lining seam allowance at the shoulder, and slipstitch it in place at the shoulder seam. Baste the lining at the neck edge and around the armscye.

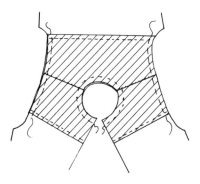

Patterns With Shaped Yokes: Baste and machine stitch the yokes in place on the front and back of the jacket. Baste and machine stitch the shoulder seams of the jacket.

Turn under the seam allowance at the bottom edges of the yoke linings and baste. Stitch the yoke shoulder seams and press them open.

Position the lining inside the jacket (wrong sides together) and baste around the neck, front edge and armscye. Slipstitch the hem of the yoke linings to the yoke seam.

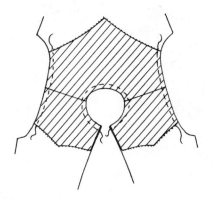

Patterns Without Yokes: Cut the pattern for the back lining so that it is 1" (25mm) wider than the jacket at the center back. This allows for a pleat at the center back of the lining. The lining should extend 3" (75mm) below the armhole at the sides.

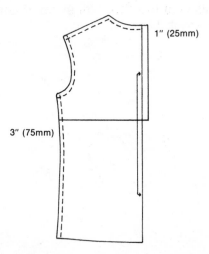

1" (25mm)

3" (75mm)

Hem the lower edge of the back lining and make a 1" (25mm) wide pleat at the center back, basting across the top and bottom. Fold under the shoulder seam allowance and baste.

Position the lining in the jacket after the shoulder and side seams have been basted and machine stitched. Baste around the armscye. Slipstitch the lining to the seam line of the garment at the shoulder and side. The lower back edge of the lining will hang free.

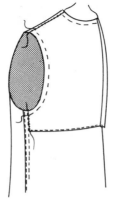

Full Linings

Fully lined jackets and coats that are hemmed at the lower edge and sleeves should have only a 1¼" (37mm) hem allowance. Adjust the pattern of both the garment and lining pieces if necessary.

The lower edge of the lining can be machine stitched to the edge of the garment hem before the front facings are stitched in place. This technique is a good one when working with Ultra Suede® fabric because hand catching the lining to the garment is somewhat difficult because of the characteristics of the suede.

Mark the hemline on the right side of the garment after all the vertical seams have been sewn but before the facing is applied. Use a chalk pencil or sliver of soap for this purpose.

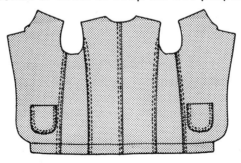

Sew the vertical seams of the lining and stitch the lining to the front facings leaving the lower 2" (5cm) unstitched.

Position the lining against the garment, right sides together, so the cut edges and seams are matched; pin in place. Stitch along the edges with a ¼" (6mm) seam leaving the first and last inch (25mm) unstitched. If the garment has a vent you must also leave an unstitched section beside each side of the vent.

Turn the lining to the inside and position the facing against the front edge of the garment as it will be for the final stitching. Fold up the garment edge along the marked hemline and hand tack at the vertical seamlines, or fuse in place using 1" (25mm) wide strips of fusible web. Pin the top edge of the lining to the neckline edge of the garment. Smooth everything in place and you will see a neat fold of fabric fall into place at the lower edge of the lining. The garment hem will be finished with one or two rows of top-stitching when the facing is finally stitched in place. Hand catch the unstitched ends of the facing in place.

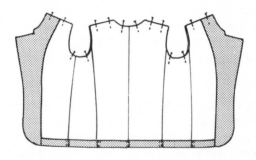

If you prefer the traditional method of hand catching the lining in place at the lower edge of the garment, machine stitch ¼" (6mm) from the hem edge before you turn the hem up and it will be much easier to catch the lining to this line of stitching than to the suede fabric itself.

Sleeve Linings

The sleeve lining will be attached to the garment at one of two points during the construction process. This is determined by the type of finish at the bottom of the sleeve. Sleeves with cuffs will have the lining attached to the lower edge of the sleeve before the cuff is applied or the sleeve is sewn into the body of the garment. Sleeves without cuffs will have the lining attached to the garment after the garment sleeve has been stitched in place.

Prepare the lining for either type of sleeve according to the following instructions. If the sleeve cap ease had to be reduced for the Ultra Suede® fabric, remember to make the same altera-tion for the lining.

Stitch and press open the underarm seam of the sleeve lining. Easestitch the cap of the sleeve ⅛" (3mm) inside the seam line, between the notches. Regular stitch the remaining armscye right on the seam line. This stitching gives a guide line on which to turn and clip the sleeve seam allowance.

Easestitching: This technique is accomplished by holding your thumb or the eraser end of a pencil on the fabric behind the presser foot as you stitch with a regular stitch length. Let the fabric pile up a bit, release, and then place your thumb or pencil back in position. You are hampering the normal feeding of the machine, and so the fabric tends to bunch up along the seam, but doesn't actually gather. Do the stitching just short of the given seamline so it won't show on the finished sleeve.

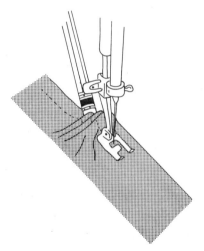

With wrong sides together, slip the lining down inside the garment sleeve. If the sleeve has a cuff finish, baste the lower edge of the sleeve and lining together. This edge will later be enclosed between the two layers of cuff fabric.

If the sleeve has a hemmed finish, the lower edge of the lining will be left free at this point but then slipstitched to the sleeve hem during the finishing of the garment.

Finish the top of the sleeve lining by turning under the seam allowance all around the sleeve edge, clipping to the seamline where necessary. Mark the notches around the edge of the sleeve with a chalk pencil so that you can distinguish them from your clips. Pin the folded edge of the sleeve to the armscye seamline of the garment and slipstitch in place.

When attaching the sleeve lining to the lower edge of the sleeve do yourself a favor by machine stitching around the edge of the garment hem at ¼" (6mm) before you turn the hem up in position. If you are using a faced finish at the edge of the sleeve, machine stitch ¼" (6mm) from the upper edge of the facing before applying the facing to the sleeve.

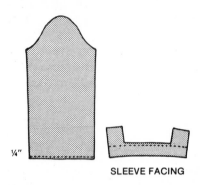

¼"

SLEEVE FACING

Finish the lining by folding under and basting ¼" (6mm) of the sleeve lining. Position the folded edge along the line of machine stitching and hand catch the fold just to the threads of the stitching line rather than trying to catch it to the Ultra Suede® fabric.

A quick and easy technique for fully lined garments is to machine stitch the sleeve lining to the body lining before putting the lining into the garment. This saves a lot of hand work.

FRONT FACINGS

Baste a strip of woven interfacing or color-matched lining fabric to the wrong side of the garment, underneath the buttonhole area, before you apply the front facings to coats and jackets. This will stabilize the buttonholes.

After the garment hem has been turned up, but before the shoulder seams are sewn, position the front facing against the garment front, wrong sides together. Remember the garment front has no seam allowance but the facing has a ⅛" (3mm) seam allowance remaining, so let the facing extend out beyond the garment edge ⅛" (3mm). Baste in place (the glue stick is a must here), and topstitch the garment fronts and hem edge with two rows of stitching, each done from the same direction. Finish the two lines of stitching at the top of the lapel as shown. Trim the facing close to the finished edge of the garment front.

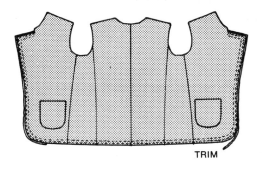

TRIM

FRONT BANDS

Baste or glue a strip of woven interfacing or color-matched lining fabric to the wrong side of the front band in the buttonhole area. Or you may want to use a strip of fusible web instead. Fusible web cut ¼" (6mm) narrower than band gives crispness to bands (and cuffs) and stabilizes buttonholes. It also eliminates any possibility of "drag" developing between rows of stitching.

Faced Bands

Mark the seamline on the front edge of the garment with pins or a sliver of soap. Lap the band piece over the front edge of the garment to the seam line. Baste or glue in place.

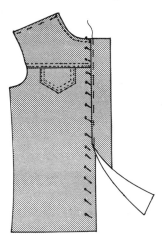

Pin and baste the band-facing in position so that ⅛" (3mm) of facing extends beyond the edge of the top piece. Working on the right side of the garment, stitch both layers of the band to the garment with two rows of topstitching.

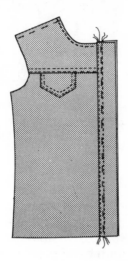

Pull apart the two layers of band and trim the garment seam allowance. This trimming must be done at this point—you can't get to it later.

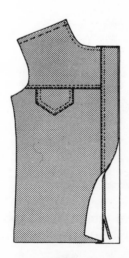

Baste the outside edges of the band together. The topstitching along the outside edge is done after the collar has been applied.

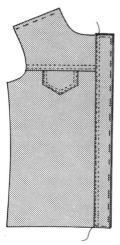

Bands With A Cut-On Facing

Mark the seamline on the front edge of the garment with pins or a sliver of soap. Lap the band piece over the front edge of the garment to the seamline. Baste or glue in place and stitch at 5/16" (7mm). Trim the seam allowance of the garment front to ¼" (6mm).

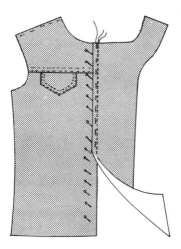

Fold the facing portion of the band back in position along the front foldline and baste again right next to the first line of basting. Edgestitch the band and facing to the garment front with one row of topstitching.

If fusible web is being used, position it in place, fold the facing, and fuse, thus eliminating the basting along the edge.

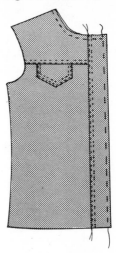

Baste along the folded edge of the facing. This edge will be topstitched after the collar has been applied.

COLLARS

Most jackets or coats you make from Ultra Suede® fabric will have a collar of some kind. The two main types of collars that you will find are collars with a separate band, and collars without bands or collars with a cut-on band. These last two collars will be applied to the garment with the same technique.

A garment having a collar with a separate band will usually have a front band finish, and the collar is applied after the shoulder seams have been sewn but before the garment side seams have been stitched. The garment calling for a collar without a band or with a cut-on band will usually have a separate front facing. The facing should be applied after the side seams are sewn but before the shoulder seams are stitched; then the shoulder seams are sewn and the collar is applied to the neck edge.

Collar With A Separate Band

Trim the seam allowances of the collar and stand pieces as given in the Cutting The Fabric section on page 31. Interface the upper collar and the inner band if you want a crisp, structured look. You can even interface both band pieces if you want a very stiff finish. Do not apply interfacing if you want a soft look.

Remember to trim the interfacing ⅛" (3mm) smaller than the Ultra Suede fabric pieces so that it will not peek out from between the layers of the finished collar.

If you are lining the garment, the lining should be basted in place around the neck edge before you apply the collar. The neck edge should also be staystitched just inside the seamline and then trimmed to ⅜" (9mm). Be sure to transfer neckline notches before trimming.

Collar Construction: Baste and double topstitch the upper and under collar together around the three outside edges. The under collar should extend ⅛" (3mm) beyond the upper collar edges at this point. Trim the under collar even with the upper collar after stitching.

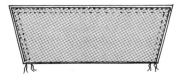

Topstitching Tip: When topstitching at collar and lapel points, insert a threaded needle through the point of the collar or lapel and use this "handle" to help pull the fabric under the presser foot as you stitch around the point. The machine tends to lose traction here and might begin to stitch in place, ruining your topstitching. Also, do not pivot the collar around the needle until it is emerging rather than going down into the fabric. This will avoid that pesky skipped stitch at the collar point.

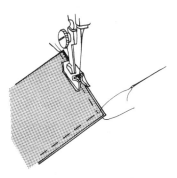

Mark the seam allowance on the lower collar edge. Pin and baste the trimmed band to the collar unit—overlapping the cut edge of the inside band to the collar seam. Baste, using a large backstitch to hold everything securely.

If fusible web is desired in the collar band, cut it ⅛" (3mm) smaller around all edges than the trimmed band piece and position it on the wrong side of the band. Handle it as one with the collar band in the following steps, hand basting if necessary.

Mark the neckline seam on the wrong side of the outside band piece.

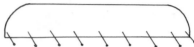

Lay the trimmed band and collar unit on top of the outside band so that the trimmed lower edge of the band is right along the marked seamline. Pin in place and baste securely across the top of the band right next to the previous basting. Hand baste in this area—the glue stick is not strong enough to hold this securely for stitching. The final topstitching that joins the collar and band will be done when the front edge of the jacket is topstitched.

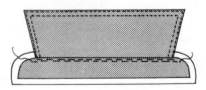

The collar is now sandwiched between the two band pieces. Pull these two pieces apart and trim the collar seam allowance to ¼" (6mm). You will not be able to get in to trim this seam once the collar has been stitched in place.

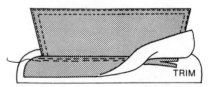

Collar Application: Clip the neckline seam to the staystitching at regular intervals as needed, and trim to ⅜" (9mm).

Pin the inside band to the neck edge so that the trimmed lower edge of the band overlaps the staystitching ⅛" (3mm). Hand baste securely in place. Now position the outside band on the neck edge so that the wrong side of the band is against the right side of the garment. Make sure both bands lie smoothly and hand baste in place. If fusible web has been used in the band, fuse the band layers together at this point, thus eliminating the basting step. It also eliminates any possibility of drag when the final rows of topstitching are done on the garment.

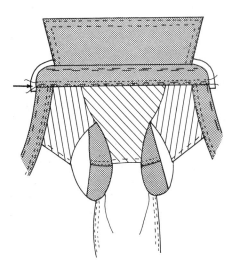

Finish the hem of the garment (see page 91) and then double topstitch the front edge and the band-collar joining seam in one operation. Trim the collar edges even, and remove any basting.

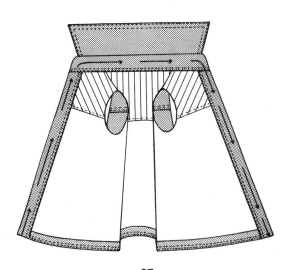

Collar Without A Band

The seam allowance of the two collar pieces should be trimmed as given on page 30. Interface the upper collar or not, as you desire. Remember to cut the interfacing ⅛" (3mm) smaller all around. Interface the under collar as given on page 18, trimming the interfacing ¼/" (6mm) smaller around the stitching lines of the three outside edges.

If you are lining the garment, the lining must be basted in place around the neck edge before you apply the collar. The neck edge should also be stay-stitched just inside the seamline and clipped at regular intervals. Do not trim the seam allowance at this time.

Draw a line marking the width of the neckline seam allowance on the wrong side of the lower edge of the upper collar.

Apply a thin strip of glue to the wrong side of the neckline edge of the collar and position the collar against the neckline seam allowance matching up construction marks and making sure the cut edge of the neckline seam meets the drawn line. Hand baste along the lower edge of the collar if you feel it is necessary.

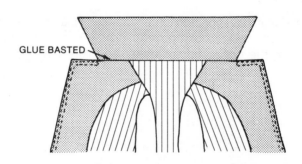

GLUE BASTED

Pin the under collar to the upper collar, wrong sides together, with ⅝" (16mm) of the under collar extending beyond the edges of the upper collar. Pin and baste or glue the neck edge of the under collar securely in position. Working on the inside of the garment, edgestitch through all layers along the lower trimmed edge of the upper collar. Only one row of stitching is done here.

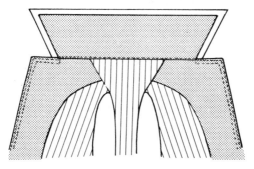

Unpin the outside edges of the collar and separate the two layers. Trim the seam allowance at the neckline. Also, trim the under collar neckline seam allowance.

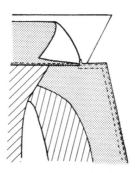

Roll the collar over your hand into the finished position and pin the two collar layers as they fall. If you have a dress form, or if you have someone to help you fit the garment on yourself you can get the proper collar roll that way. You will notice that you may have more than ⅝" (16mm) of the under collar extending beyond the edge of the upper collar at this point. This is the natural shortening of the under collar and is what creates a nice rolled collar that stays flat and neat around your neck.

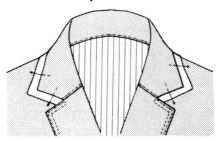

While the collar is still in the rolled position, glue the edges together; then finish with two rows of topstitching. The stitching pattern should look like this:

Collar With Cut-On Band

Use the above techniques for applying the collar with a cut-on band with the option of doing two rows of topstitching where the collar joins the neckline edge instead of one row.

SLEEVE VENTS

The finish at the bottom of the sleeve will, of course, be determined by your pattern. Some sleeves will have a faced vent such as found on men's suits; some will require a vent finish combined with a cuff, and some sleeves will just have a simple hemmed edge. Read through these instructions and combine them with your pattern requirements for the desired finish.

Sleeve vents are constructed before the underarm seam of the sleeve is sewn unless the vent is part of that seam.

Slash Vent

Cut a vent facing from Ultra Suede® fabric that is 3" (76mm) wide and 1" (25mm) longer than the vent slash. Slash the sleeve along the vent marking, rounding the top of the slash.

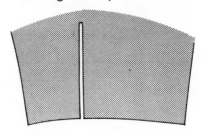

Pin and baste the facing in the proper position wrong sides together. Make two rows of stitching around the vent slash, as illustrated.

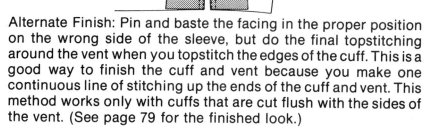

Alternate Finish: Pin and baste the facing in the proper position on the wrong side of the sleeve, but do the final topstitching around the vent when you topstitch the edges of the cuff. This is a good way to finish the cuff and vent because you make one continuous line of stitching up the ends of the cuff and vent. This method works only with cuffs that are cut flush with the sides of the vent. (See page 79 for the finished look.)

Stitch the underarm seam using either the conventional or lapped seam method. If the garment is going to be lined, the sleeve lining should be stitched now and slipped down inside the garment sleeve, wrong sides together. Slash the lining along the vent line cutting it ½" (13mm) longer than the pattern indicated. Slip the lining behind the vent facing and slipstitch in place. Baste the lower edge of the sleeve and lining together.

Tailored Vent

Slash the sleeve on the vent marking making the slash 4½" (113cm) long. Face the back of the vent (the edge closest to the underarm seam) with a ¾" (19mm) wide strip of Ultra Suede® fabric that is cut 5" (13cm) long. Baste and double topstitch in place as illustrated.

71

Cut a sleeve placket piece from Ultra Suede fabric using the pattern found in the back of the book. Cut ⅜" (9mm) into the sleeve at the top of the vent.

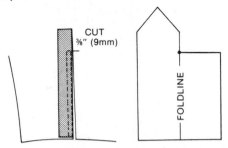

Fold the vent facing in half, wrong sides together. Baste and double topstitch the folded edge to the dot. Pull the threads through to the inside of the two layers and tie.

Working on the right side of the sleeve, sandwich the edge of the sleeve-slash in between the unstitched edges of the vent facing, overlapping the sleeve edge ⅜" (9mm). The lower edge of the vent facing should be even with the lower edge of the sleeve. Baste in position and double topstitch as shown.

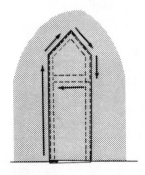

Stitch the underarm seam and apply any sleeve lining as described in the previous vent section.

Vent In A Seam

Some patterns will have a sleeve vent constructed as part of the sleeve seam. You will find this type of construction more often on men's than on women's garments. It is a very easy vent finish, and you can modify any sleeve pattern to use this type of vent if you wish by following the instruction below.

Draw a line up the back section of the sleeve starting where the vent slash is located. Cut the sleeve apart along this line and add a ⅝" (16mm) seam allowance to both sides of the cut, plus an extra ½" (13mm) in the vent area.

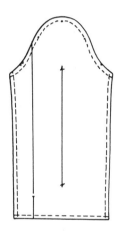

Now overlap the original underarm seam so that the seam lines are on top of each other. Tape in place and use this new pattern to cut your sleeves.

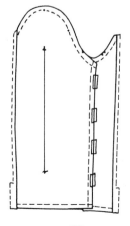

Baste, stitch and press open the underarm seam of the sleeve. Use thin strips of fusible web under the seam allowances to hold them flat, or edgestitch on each side of the seam.

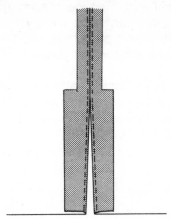

When you line this type of sleeve, you should cut the lining from the altered sleeve pattern. Stitch the underarm seam to a point ½" (13mm) above the top of the vent opening and press the seam open. Slip the lining down inside the sleeve and baste along the lower edge. Slipstitch the edge of the lining to the vent edges.

Faced Vent

A tailored sleeve vent on a man's sport coat or woman's jacket is best handled with a facing. Cut the facing as follows:

Overlap the sleeve pattern pieces at the front seam until the seamlines are on top of each other; pin together. Remove the hem allowance from both sleeve pattern pieces and the vent extension of the upper sleeve. Trace around this adjusted pattern for your sleeve facing, making it ⅛" (3mm) larger around the three outside edges, 3" (7.5cm) wide on the sides of the vent, and 2" (5cm) wide at the bottom edge. Note: be sure sleeve is correct length as you cannot adjust later.

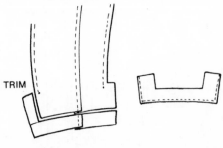

TRIM

Stitch the front seam of the sleeve using either the conventional or flat technique.

Apply interfacing to the sleeve facing if more body is desired. Cut the interfacing ¼" (6mm) smaller than the facing so it doesn't peek out from the finished sleeve. Also, machine stitch ¼" (6mm) down from the edge of the facing so you will have a line of stitching for attaching the lining.

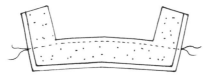

Position the facing against the lower edge of the sleeve, wrong sides together and glue. Remember the facing is ⅛" (3mm) larger than the sleeve so it should extend out beyond the sleeve edge that much. Double topstitch around the facing as shown. End the stitching at the construction dot marking the top of the vent. Pull the threads through to the wrong side and tie. Trim the excess facing.

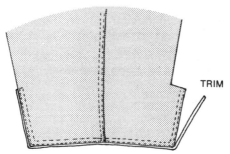

TRIM

Baste and stitch the upper sleeve seam to the dot, using the lapped seam method. This works best if the sleeve is turned inside out for the stitching. Stitch both seams from the same direction. Hold the vent closed by sewing the vent buttons in place.

Many women cringe at the prospect of stitching "inside the tube" for the sleeve faced vent finish on page 233 of **Sew Smart**. As an alternative, when cutting the sleeves, remove ONLY the upper sleeve vent-side seam allowance.

Make the vent facing pattern as shown on page 233 of **Sew Smart.** Interface the facing for more body. (No more curled up corners at the vent.) Position the facing against the lower edge of the sleeve, wrong sides together and baste. Remember, the facing is 1/8" larger than the sleeve so it should extend out beyond the sleeve edge that much. Double topstitch the vent, stopping 1" from the front edge as shown. Bring thread ends to the wrong side and knot.

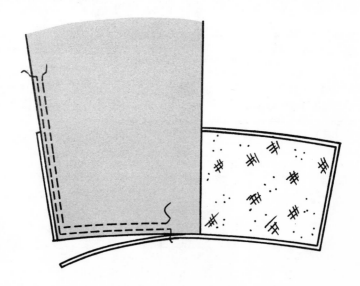

Lap the upper sleeve over the under sleeve seam allowance at the vent, baste and stitch. Start stitching precisely where the vent stitching stopped.

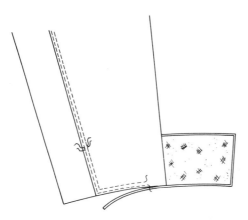

Close the remaining sleeve seam with a conventional 5/8'' seam allowance. Press open. Turn right side out. Baste the partially stitched vent facing to the remainder of the sleeve and finish the 2 rows of topstitching. Trim off the excess facing and breathe a sigh of relief!

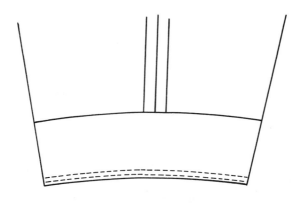

CUFFS

Directions are given for the two basic types of cuffs you will find on patterns, the cuff with a separate facing and the one-piece fold-over cuff. Interfacing the cuff is optional. If you decide to use it, apply the interfacing to the upper cuff piece or the half of the fold-over cuff which will form the upper cuff. Remember to trim the interfacing ⅛" (3mm) smaller than the cuff so that it won't peek out around the edges.

Fusible web, cut to fit the finished cuff, can be used instead of interfacing, if desired. It gives a crisp look and eliminates any chance of drag when sewing the final rows of topstitching. Glue baste it in position before you begin the cuff application.

If you choose not to use interfacing or fusible web, then position a patch of color matched, woven lining fabric under the button-hole area for support. Glue will hold the patch in place until the buttonhole is worked.

Cuff With A Separate Facing

The upper cuff piece should be trimmed of all seam allowances. The cuff facing should retain the full seam allowance at the sleeve edge and just a ⅛" (3mm) seam allowance around the outer three edges.

Position the lining in the sleeve and baste around the lower edge. Mark the seamline at the lower edge of the sleeve. Lap the upper cuff over the seam allowance so that the trimmed edge just meets the seamline. Baste or glue in position.

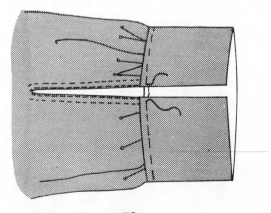

Position the cuff facing under the cuff, wrong sides together, so that ⅛" (3mm) of the facing extends beyond the three outside edges of the upper cuff. Baste or glue securely at the sleeve edge. Double topstitch through all layers at the top edge of the cuff.

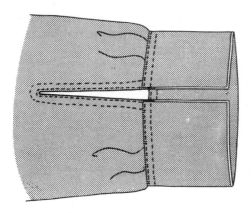

Separate the cuff pieces and trim the sleeve seam allowance. Trim away the excess seam allowance at the sleeve edge of the cuff facing also.

Baste the outer edges of the cuff and facing together. If fusible web has been used in the cuff, fuse the cuff layers together at this point, eliminating the basting step. Double topstitch around the three outer edges.

Trim the facing even with the upper cuff edge. Do both lines of stitching from the same direction.

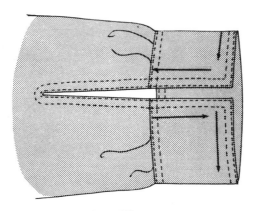

Fold-Over Cuff

This cuff piece should have three seam allowances trimmed away, leaving just one intact at the sleeve edge.

Mark the seamline on the right side of the lower edge of the sleeve. Lap the trimmed edge of the cuff over the lower sleeve seam until the edge meets the seamline. Baste or glue in place. Trim away ¼" (6mm) of the sleeve seam allowance at the lower edge of the sleeve.

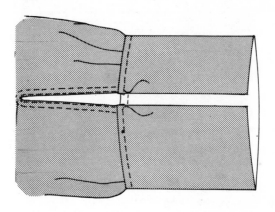

Fold the facing portion of the cuff back in the finished position, wrong sides together. The ⅝" (16mm) seam allowance will extend up into the sleeve. Baste across the top of the cuff again and then baste or glue around all three outside edges. This basting is important in order to prevent the layers of fabric from shifting during the final stitching. If fusible web has been used in the cuff this is the time to fuse the cuff layer together, thus eliminating the basting.

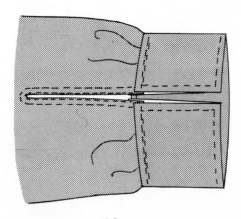

Double topstitch across the top of the cuff. Double topstitch around the outside edges of the cuff. It is important that these two stitching operations be done from the same direction so that a "drag" does not develop around the cuff edge. Trim away excess seam allowance at the top edge of the cuff facing.

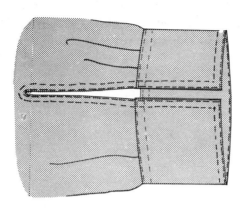

SETTING IN SLEEVES

Always set sleeves into the armhole with a conventional seam. This method is easiest and looks best when finished.

Remember to check and adjust the sleeve cap ease before cutting out the sleeve, as directed on page 35.

The remaining 1" (25mm) of ease must be controlled some way while you stitch the sleeve in place, and we have found this to be the easiest method.

To control sleeve cap ease on stiff or densely woven fabrics such as Ultrasuede, denim or corduroy use a strip of wide Seams Great as an "ease strip". Measure the garmet armscye from notch to notch.

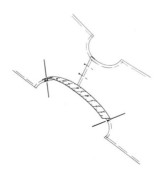

Cut the wide (1¼") Seams Great 1" longer than this measurement. The extra 1" gives a ½" handle to hold onto at each end of the "ease strip". Stretch and stitch the "ease strip" to the sleeve cap just inside the seam allowance so the stitches won't show. Now the sleeve can be stitched into the garment without tell-tale puckers that ruin the smooth look that you want. The "ease strip" controls the ease in the dense fabric. No need to trim away the "ease strip" as it helps fill in the sleeve cap area.

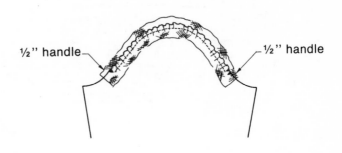

½" handle   ½" handle

Pin the sleeve into the armhole, matching the construction marks. Place the pins directly in the seamline for better control of the fabric ease. Baste in place and try the garment on to check the fit.

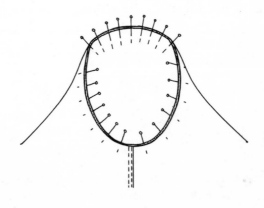

Once the fit is perfect and smooth, machine stitch the sleeve in place. Stitch a second row ¼'' (6mm) in the seam allowance. Trim to this stitching. Tailored jackets and coats look nicer if you add a shoulder pad; casual jackets can also have a shoulder pad if desired.

Position a shoulder pad in the garment so the edge of the pad meets the trimmed edge of the armscye seam allowance when it is turned out into the sleeve. Catch in place at the ends and center of the shoulder pad, making sure the stitches go only through the seam allowance. Tack the inside edge of the pad to the shoulder seam allowance.

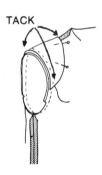

TACK

ZIPPERS

Some Ultra Suede fabric garments will require zippers, and these are really very easy to insert. Zippers in conventional seams will be stitched in using the traditional techniques. However, the flat method of seam construction makes it possible to easily insert zippers that have a very flat finish. Follow the instructions below for the center-slot, lapped and fly zipper.

Center-Slot Zipper

The simplest way to insert the center-slot zipper in an Ultra Suede fabric garment is to use Flat Seam II method for the zipper seam.

Trim the seam allowance from both sides of the seam. Cut a 1'' (25mm) wide strip of fabric the same length as the seam. Butt the trimmed edges of the seam together and center them down the length of the strip. Baste in place and edgestitch each side of the seam.

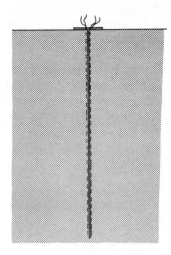

Make a slash down the center of the 1" (25mm) wide strip the length of the zipper. Position the zipper under the slash and baste or glue securely.

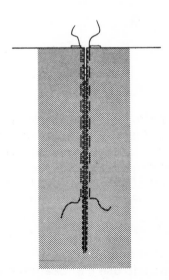

Do the second row of topstitching ¼" (6mm) away from the first, stitching from the same direction on each side. This row of stitching holds the zipper in place, and you will have four neat rows of topstitching showing down the zipper seam.

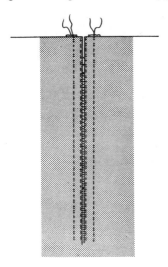

Lapped Zipper

This method is used at the sides of skirts and pants and at the center back of pants, skirts and dresses. It is also a simple way of making a fly zipper for pants. Just add two extra rows of topstitching to outline the fly.

Trim the seam allowance from the edge of the garment that laps over the zipper. Trim the other seam allowance a scant ⅜" (13mm) just the length of the zipper.

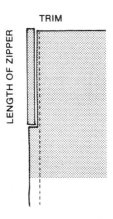

TRIM

LENGTH OF ZIPPER

Zipper Tip: Use a longer zipper than necessary so it extends entirely above the waistline seam. This makes it easier to lower the back waistline seam if necessary for fitting purposes. You won't be cutting into the metal stoppers at the top of the zipper.

Position the zipper under the partially trimmed garment pieces so the fabric edge is next to the zipper teeth. Glue or baste in place and edgestitch with a zipper foot the length of the zipper teeth.

Cut a facing for the other side of the garment that is 1" (25mm) wide and 1" (25mm) longer than the zipper. Lay the facing along the edge of the completely trimmed seam allowance, wrong sides together. Glue or baste and double topstitch the edge of the facing just the length of the zipper.

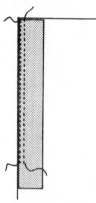

Mark the seamline down the length of the garment piece to which the zipper has been attached. Lap the faced side of the garment over the zipper so that the trimmed edge meets the seamline.

Baste in position. Double topstitch the remainder of the seam below the zipper.

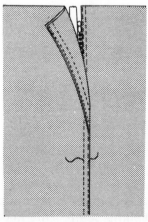

Working on the right side of the garment, fold back the side until the zipper facing is exposed. Baste the facing to the zipper tape. Machine stitch the facing to the zipper tape with a row of machine stitching.

Slip a ¼" (6mm) strip of fusible web in between the facing and garment fabric. Fuse in place from the wrong side. This keeps the facing flat and always in the right position.

Fly Zippers

Trim away the seam allowance on the lapped over part of the garment and leave the seam allowance completely intact on the under part of the garment.

Position the zipper under the edge of the untrimmed seam allowance so the edge of the fabric is beside the zipper teeth. Glue or baste and edgestitch with a zipper foot, close to the zipper teeth.

Cut a facing for the other side of the garment that is 2" (5cm) wide and 1" (25mm) longer than the zipper. Lay the facing along the edge of the other seam, wrong sides together. Glue or baste and double topstitch the edge of the facing just the length of the zipper.

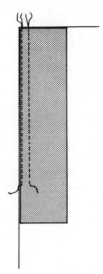

Mark the seamline down the length of the garment piece to which the zipper has been attached. Lay the faced side of the garment over the zipper so that the trimmed edge meets the marked seamline. Glue or baste and double topstitch the remainder of the seam below the zipper.

Working on the right side of the garment, fold back the garment until the zipper facing is exposed. Hand or glue baste the facing to the zipper tape and then machine stitch together.

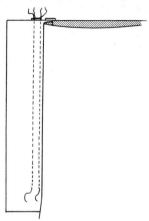

Slip a ½" (13mm) wide strip of fusible web in between the facing and garment fabric. Fuse in place from the wrong side.

Finish the fly zipper with two rows of decorative topstitching 1¼" (31mm) from the edge on the right side of the garment. This stitching should also catch the zipper tape.

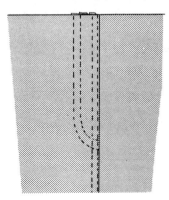

WAISTBANDS

You will find two types of waistbands on Ultra Suede® fabric garments, the faced waistband and the fold-over waistband. Fold-over waistbands use larger pieces of fabric than faced waistbands, so if you are short of large, un-cut pieces of fabric, you can make the waistband into a faced one and utilize smaller pieces of fabric. Just cut the waistband pattern apart along the foldline and use these two pieces to cut the waistband and facing.

Interface waistbands that are used at the top of pants and skirts, or eliminate the interfacing and just don't trim the waistline seam; it will act as interfacing. Interfacing is optional for waistbands at the bottom edge of jackets, or you can use a piece of fusible web between the waistband layer for a crisp look. In either case, a piece of woven interfacing or color-matched lining fabric should be positioned on the wrong side of the band underneath the buttonhole area.

Faced Waistbands

The upper waistband piece should have all the seam allowances trimmed away. The waistband facing should have the three out-side seam allowances trimmed to ⅛" (3mm); the seam allowance that joins the body of the garment should be left intact.

Mark the seamline on the right side of the garment piece that joins the waistband. Overlap the upper waistband piece until the trimmed edge meets the seamline. Baste or glue securely in place.

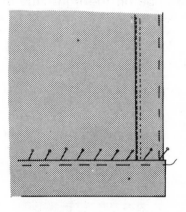

Position the waistband facing against the upper waistband, wrong sides together. The ⅛" (3mm) allowance of the facing should extend beyond the edges of the upper waistband. Baste or glue in place and then finish with a double row of topstitching. Separate the two waistband layers and trim the seam allowance.

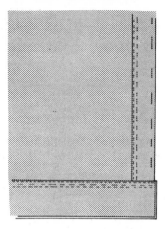

Pin and baste or glue the edges of the waistband together. Or a piece of fusible web cut ¼" (6mm) narrower than the waistband can be fused in place between the fabric layers and fused together at this point. Double topstitch the remaining edges of the waistband. If the garment has a collar and front facing or band that hasn't been topstitched, then continue the topstitching through these areas at this time. Make sure that all the rows of topstitching are made in the same direction.

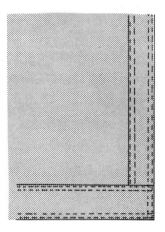

Fold-Over Waistbands

Use the pattern piece given with the pattern, or, if you are making a waistband for pants or a skirt, cut the waistband piece 1" (25mm) longer than the top edge of the garment and 2½" (64mm) wide.

The 1" (25mm) band extension can be placed on either side of the waist opening, as you prefer.

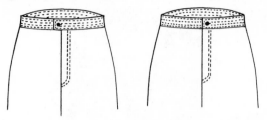

Mark the seamline at the waist of the garment and lap the waistband to the seamline. Baste or glue in position.

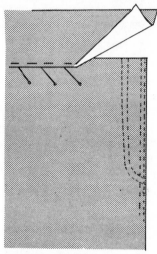

Fold the waistband down in the finished position so that ½" (13mm) extends below the waistline seam on the wrong side. Baste or glue securely. Note: The waistline seam is left untrimmed in the waistband to give extra body. Fusible web can be added to the waistband also if desired.

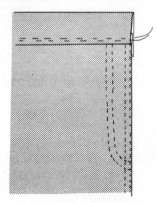

Finish the waistband by making four rows of topstitching along the length of the waistband. Make sure that all the rows of stitching are done from the same direction. Trim the front edges of the waistband even and trim away the excess seam allowance from the back of the band.

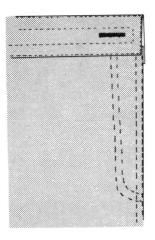

HEMS

If you look at ready-to-wear Ultra Suede® fabric garments you will see various types of hem finishes. Some garments are just cut at the desired length and left with a raw edge. We feel this gives an unfinished look and encourage you to make conventional or faced hems.

Conventional Hems

Turn up the garment along the hemline. The hem width is ¾" (19mm) for unlined garments and 1¼" (31mm) for lined garments. The hem allowance of the pattern should be trimmed to these widths before being pinned to the fabric.

Finish the hem by fusing with strips of fusible web or making a double row of topstitching along the lower edge. A word of caution here, fused hems sometimes get a "glued look" after repeated washings.

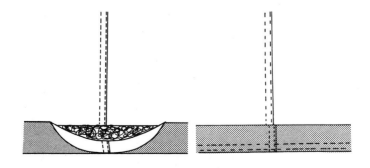

Hems can also be done by hand. Do a row of machine stitching ¼" below the hem edge first and catch the hand stitches to this stitching line instead of the suede. Much easier.

Clotilde prefers the hand blindstitch hem for a more dressy look. It leaves no line of demarcation on the right side. This conventional hem can be 1" to 2" wide --- and, this gives you the option of lowing the hem at a later date.

Pin the hem in place, and roll back the hem edge ¼". Working from right to left, catch several threads of the rolled-back hem. Next, insert the needle just behind the thread and take a small stitch that won't show on the right side of the garment; cross over the thread and insert the needle in the hem fold about ½" to the left.

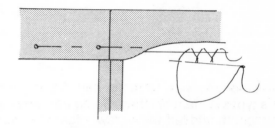

Faced Hems

Faced hems are more suitable for garments with curved edges. It is impossible to use a conventional hem finish on these garments and achieve a smooth look since Ultra Suede fabric does not ease well.

Cut facing strips ¾" (19mm) wide, using the garment piece as a pattern so that you duplicate the curve exactly. Position the facing against the garment, wrong sides together, and baste or glue. Finish with a double row of topstitching along the lower edge.

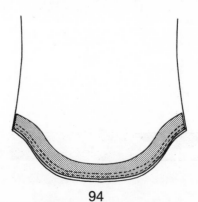

Hems At The Front Facing

Garments that are hemmed and have a fold-back or separate front facing should be finished according to the following instructions.

Conventional Hem: Fold the hem up and baste or glue. Trim the front edge of the hem so that it extends only ½″ (13mm) into the facing. Fold the facing back in the finished position. Baste or glue in position and trim after it has been stitched across the lower edge.

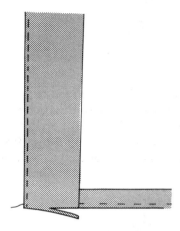

Finish the lower edge by fusing the hem with strips of fusible web or double topstitching along the lower edge of the hem. If you are topstitching the hem edge, then topstitch the entire jacket at this time, going up the fronts, across the collar and across the bottom edges in one operation. Make both rows of stitching from the same direction.

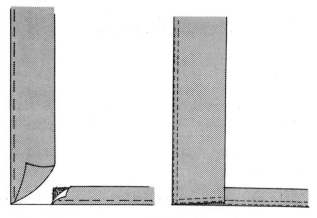

Faced Hem: The lower edge of the facing should be trimmed ⅛"
(3mm) wider than the lower edge of the garment.

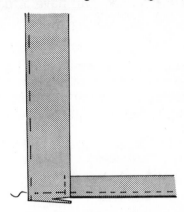

Face the hem with a ¾" (19mm) wide strip of Ultra Suede® fabric
placed wrong sides together with the facing extending ⅛" (3mm)
below the garment edge. The hem strip should extend just ½"
(13mm) into the facing at the front edge. Baste or glue the hem
facing in place and finish by double topstitching as above. Trim
all edges even.

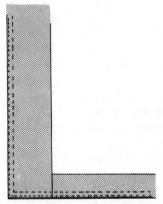

BUTTONHOLES

All buttonholes should be backed by interfacing to prevent rippling and stretching. A square or strip of woven interfacing, or
better yet, a color-matched lining fabric should be used. Color-
matched lining will avoid having a strip of white showing in the
buttonhole opening.

There are four methods of making buttonholes in Ultra Suede

fabric. All are easy, but the bound buttonhole does require precise marking and cutting. It is suggested that you try the various buttonhole methods on scraps of fabric to see which one works best for you. You will also work out any construction problems before you begin work on the garment.

Buttonhole I

This is the easiest buttonhole and is frequently seen on Designer fashions.

Using 14 stitches to the inch (or a stitch length of 2mm), stitch a rectangle the desired length and ⅛" (3mm) wide at each buttonhole location. Count the stitches along each side to make sure all the buttonholes are the same size. Cut the buttonholes open using an Exacto knife, buttonhole cutter, or a single-edged razor blade.

Buttonhole II

Do a regular machine buttonhole. These look best when corded. See your machine instruction book for cording instructions.

Buttonhole III

This is the easiest bound buttonhole, and it gives a nice flat look. Make the front part of this buttonhole before the facing is attached to the garment. If the buttonholes are being made in a front band, waistband or cuff, make the front side of the buttonholes before you attach these pieces to the garment.

Make a template the exact size of the buttonhole opening. The cardboard from bias or seam tape makes a good template. Cut the buttonhole ¼" (6mm) wide and the exact length of the buttonhole. The distance from the front edge of the buttonhole to the edge of the cardboard should be the same distance from the front edge of the buttonhole to the edge of the garment. This will make the positioning of the template easier.

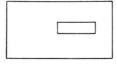

Use the template to cut the buttonhole "windows" on the garment piece. Make sure the windows are placed exactly where they are supposed to be before cutting. Use an Exacto knife, buttonhole cutter, or a single-edge razor blade to cut the openings.

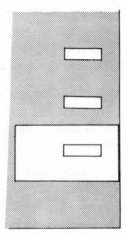

Cut two strips of fabric 1" x 2" (25mm x 50mm) for each buttonhole. (The strips should be 1" (25mm) longer than the buttonhole opening.) Place the two strips right sides together and machine baste down the center of the strips.

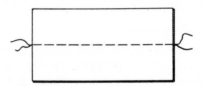

Press the strips open and position them under the buttonhole windows, centering them in the opening. Baste securely around the outside edges of the window or glue in place.

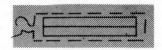

After the facing has been attached to the garment, baste or glue around the buttonhole again, through the facing layer. Finish the buttonhole by edgestitching around the buttonhole window. Use a zipper foot here for greater visibility.

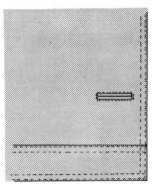

Remove any basting stitches, including the ones across the buttonhole openings, and cut a window or slit on the facing side just inside the stitched box.

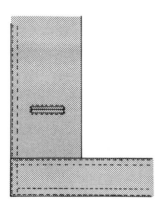

Note: Do not baste or glue the buttonhole to the facing until after the facing has been double topstitched in place. Sometimes the facing will shift a little during the topstitching and this would cause a wrinkling around the buttonhole if it had been finished.

Buttonhole IV

Because this bound buttonhole does not have any stitches visible from the right side, it is very elegant looking. Remember that the front of the buttonhole is constructed before the facing is attached to the garment.

Cut two strips of fabric 1" x 2" (25mm x 50mm) or 1" (25mm) longer than each buttonhole opening.

Mark the exact position and width of each buttonhole with a fine pencil or basting thread on the right side of the garment. Double check your marks to make sure they are accurate.

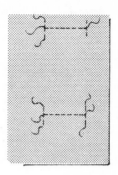

Place one buttonhole strip along the buttonhole line, right sides together, so that at least ½″ (13mm) extends beyond each end of the buttonhole. Baste and stitch ⅛″ (3mm) from the edge, the exact length of the buttonhole.

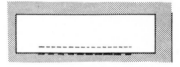

Position the second strip on the right side of the garment so that its cut edge butts against the cut edge of the first strip. Baste in position and stitch as for the first strip. It helps if you count stitches so that the stitching lines are the same length.

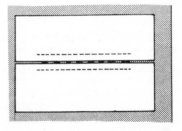

From the wrong side, cut the buttonhole open as shown, leaving a good-sized wedge at each end. Do not cut the strips of fabric—just the garment fabric.

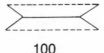

Turn the strips to the wrong side. Open the ⅛" (3mm) seam and flatten it with your fingernail. Wrap the buttonhole strips over the open seams and baste in position, as illustrated.

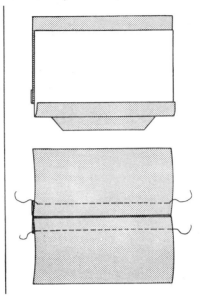

Fold back the garment at each side of the buttonhole and machine stitch across the base of each wedge.

Baste or glue and topstitch the front facing to the garment. Baste around each buttonhole going through the facing layer at this time or glue the facing in place.

Set the machine for 16 stitches to the inch (stitch length of slightly less than 2mm) and finish the buttonhole by stitching-in-the-ditch around each buttonhole. Stitch slowly, using a zipper foot for greater visibility; you don't want any of this stitching to show. Do this by hand if you can't bury stitches in the seam.

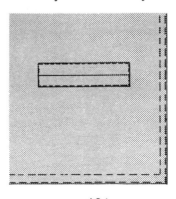

Remove all the basting and cut a window or a slit in the facing of the garment just inside the stitched box of each buttonhole.

LEFT-OVER PROJECTS

Don't throw away any of those scraps of Ultra Suede® fabric. At the price you paid, they are worth lots of money. They can be used for High-Fashion touches on other garments and clever craft projects. A few suggestions are given below. You'll probably think up more for yourself.

WRAP BELT

Cut a strip of Ultra Suede fabric across the width 3" (7.5cm) to 3½" (8.7cm) wide. Taper the ends and tie in a square knot for an instant high-fashion accent belt.

PATCHES

What can be more fun than Ultra Suede fabric patches on jeans? Use various colors, cut in exciting shapes, and you will really add a touch of class to those old favorites. Little kids love the patches on their clothes, too!

BUTTONS

Make covered buttons and use them on other garments as well as your Ultra Suede® fabric ones. They really add interest and are machine washable to boot. The buttons are easier to make if you dampen the suede fabric before putting it on the button forms.

BUTTONHOLES

Make bound buttonholes using Ultra Suede fabric for the lips. This looks especially nice on corduroy jackets. Use the buttonhole method given on page 97 (Buttonhole IV).

PIPING

Use narrow strips of Ultra Suede fabric to pipe collars, yokes, pockets, cuffs and anything else you can think of when making garments from other fabrics. Piping adds the look of real leather to the garment, giving none of the stitching and cleaning problems.

Piping Instructions

To make piping, cut ¾" (19mm) wide strips of Ultra Suede fabric on the crossgrain. Fold the strips in half, wrong sides together, and stitch ⅛" (3mm) from the fold.

Baste the strip to the garment section to be piped so that the stitching on the piping lies along the seamline on the right side of the garment. Clip the piping to the stitching when going around points, corners and curves.

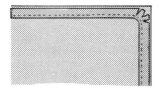

Pin the garment pieces together, right side to right side, so that the suede strip is sandwiched in between. Stitch the seam and then trim, turn and press.

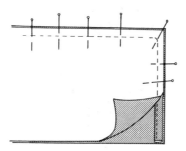

FASHION ACCENTS

Use pieces of Ultra Suede® fabric to accent patch and welt pockets. It also looks nice applied to the collars of sports coats. Make a hunting jacket by stitching Ultra Suede fabric patches to the shoulder and elbows. The shoulder patch goes on the right side unless, of course, the man is left handed.

Make a vest with an Ultra Suede® fabric front and a sweater knit back. Or stitch together patches of various colors of Ultra Suede fabric for a patchwork vest.

Design a Western scene out of Ultra Suede® fabric scraps and zigzag the pieces to the back yoke of a denim jacket. (You can buy a similar jacket in the store for $250.)

Make a braided belt from strips of suede trimmed from seams. Use the braid for a tie belt or a regular belt with a buckle. You can also hand stitch the braid to a denim work shirt or jacket for a new look.

Wide belts and purses made from Ultra Suede fabric are unusual. There are many patterns available for these.

Use small scraps for appliques or miniature patchworks. Ultra Suede fabric scraps are also great for cleaning glasses. They would even make a good eyeglass case or liner.

SWEATER TRIMS

Narrow strips of Ultra Suede fabric can be used to accent the neck and sleeve trim of men's and women's sweaters. Cut the strips ⅜" or ½" (9mm or 13mm) wide across the grain of the fabric.

Turtleneck Trim

Use a regular turtleneck sweater pattern, but cut out the entire neckline 2" (50mm) larger than the pattern requirement. This lowering allows the sweater to slip over the head after the Ultra Suede® fabric has been applied.

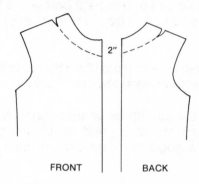

FRONT | BACK

Cut the turtleneck strip 8" (20cm) wide and long enough to stretch around the head and then fit comfortably around the neck. Stitch the narrow edges of the collar, right sides together, and then finger press the seam open. Fold the collar in half, wrong sides together; divide and mark the cut edge into four equal sections.

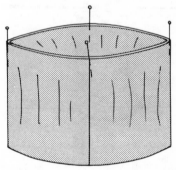

With the garment inside out, divide and mark the neckline into four equal sections. Slip the prepared collar down into the neckline and pin the edges together, matching up the quarter marks. The collar seam should be placed at the center back. Stitch the neckline with a ¼" (6mm) seam.

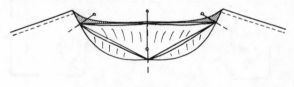

Glue baste the Ultra Suede® fabric strip to the neckline so that the lower edge runs right on the neckline seam.

Lap the edges of the strip at the center back and attach to the collar with two rows of topstitching.

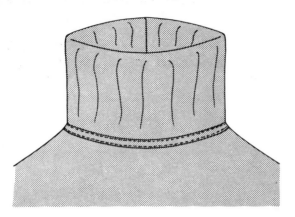

V-Neck Trim

Topstitch one or two narrow strips of Ultra Suede fabric to the band of the V-neck before it is attached to the sweater. Baste and double topstitch the strips to the neckband before you fold it into the finished position, and stitch it to the garment.

Cuff Trim

Stitch narrow strips of Ultra Suede fabric around the cuffs of sweaters to give you a complete fashion look. Apply the strips to the cuff trim before folding and applying to the sleeve opening. Be sure the cuff will go over the hand—Ultra Suede cuts down on stretch of the cuff.

There is no end to the things you can do with all those expensive scraps. Using them up is almost as exciting as making the actual garment. Have fun!

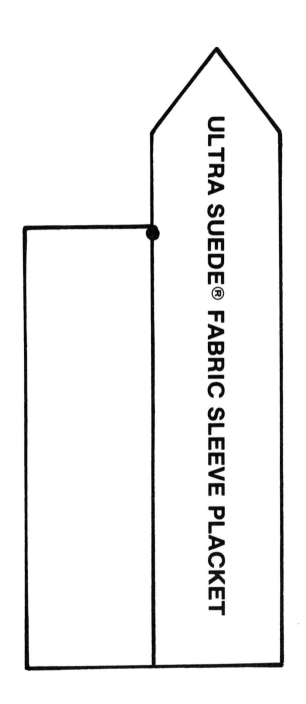

ULTRA SUEDE® FABRIC SLEEVE PLACKET